? and Miracles in the High Desert

. of her life among the Navajo people is a story of high adventure that surpasses the wildest fiction. Elliott's willingness to transcend her cultural conditioning and enter another complex society is an act of great courage—one that reveals her boundless empathy and compassion. This book is sorely needed at this moment in America, when divisive voices incessantly warn us of the other, the foreigner, those who "are not like us." *Medicine and Miracles in the High Desert: My Life Among the Navajo People* reveals how diversity and inclusiveness can enrich our own society—a lesson on which our future may depend."

—Larry Dossey, MD, author of *One Mind: How Our Individual Mind Is Part of a Greater Consciousness and Why It Matters*

"What a wonderful book! Elliott's voice mesmerized me. For weeks after I read this, I thought about her time with the Navajos. Such an inspiring, life-affirming, yet tough tale, woven through with a strong drive to realize her life path. Beautifully written. Elliott is an exciting new voice."

—Natalie Goldberg, author of *Writing Down the Bones* and *Let the Whole Thundering World Come Home*

"Erica Elliott writes fearlessly, with an original voice that grabbed me from the first page. Her true adventures on the Navajo Nation as a teacher, a shepherd, an emergency room doctor—and best of all, an open-hearted student immersed in a spiritually rich culture—make a great story. She leaves the reader with something to ponder: The abiding importance of reaching out to others with joy and respect. I love this book."

—Anne Hillerman, *NY Times* bestselling author of the Leaphorn, Chee, and Manuelito mystery series

"This is a powerful and personal book about courage and compassion. Reading it, we are drawn into the web of Dr. Elliott's extraordinary life of service and learning with the Navajo people of the American Southwest. We are fortunate for the chance to accompany her on her remarkable journey."

—Rev. Joan Jiko Halifax, Abbot of Upaya Zen Center
and author of *Standing at the Edge*

Medicine and Miracles

in the High Desert

My Life Among the Navajo People

ERICA M. ELLIOTT, M.D.

BALBOA.
PRESS

A DIVISION OF HAY HOUSE

Balboa Press books may be ordered through booksellers or by contacting:

Balboa Press
A Division of Hay House
1663 Liberty Drive
Bloomington, IN 47403
www.balboapress.com
1 (877) 407-4847

Print information available on the last page.

ISBN: 978-1-9822-2098-3 (sc)
ISBN: 978-1-9822-2097-6 (hc)
ISBN: 978-1-9822-2105-8 (e)

Library of Congress Control Number: 2019901055

Balboa Press rev. date: 02/15/2019

This book is dedicated to the *Diné*, who invited me into their homes and into their hearts and showed me a whole different way of living that powerfully transformed my life.

CONTENTS

FOREWORD

by Joan Borysenko, Ph.D.

I want to tell you a story about the author of this enchanted tale, Erica Elliott, M.D., before I introduce you to her memoir.

Several months before this book was to be published, Erica and I were walking together companionably on a clear summer's day. The wide azure sky of New Mexico stretched endlessly above us, and a dry riverbed carpeted with rocks and sand meandered below. Feet clad in sturdy hiking shoes, I picked my way along gingerly, wary of the ubiquitous cactus thorns and whatever desert denizens might have emerged to sunbathe. Erica, herself a denizen of the high desert, gamboled along the arroyo barefoot and as carefree as anyone could be while awaiting hip surgery.

I was amazed. But that's how you always feel when you're with Erica. She's so humble that it's easy to be blindsided by her accomplishments—whether it's hearing her speak Navajo or one of the other half-dozen or so languages she has picked up, or discussing the fine points of science and medicine, or marveling at her strength and easy athleticism. A skier, rafter, and climber, Erica led an all-women's expedition to the top of Denali, aka Mt. McKinley, in 1980. Four years before, she had become the first American woman to climb Aconcagua in Argentina, the highest mountain in the Western Hemisphere.

ix

Believe me, this woman has grit.

Walking along, stopping often to face each other in delight, we discussed which of the several books that Erica is planning to write should come first. Perhaps the story of how she became seriously ill after prolonged exposure to chemicals in the clinic where she was practicing mainstream medicine?

Back then, in the early Nineties, awareness of environmental sensitivities was in its infancy. All too often, physicians told patients like Erica, "It's all in your head," or "Try to relax—you're just stressed out."

I know firsthand what it was like in those days, since I was the director of a mind-body clinic at one of Harvard Medical School's teaching hospitals. When docs couldn't help environmentally sensitive patients, they sent them to me. I never believed that the variety of symptoms such patients experienced—from fatigue and brain fog to respiratory problems, nausea, headache, autoimmune conditions, and neurological problems, to name a few—were all psychosomatic. Without question, our environment was becoming more toxic by the day.

Erica, who is a brilliant scientist, was a canary in a coalmine. She was among those in the first wave of environmentally induced illnesses. A single mom struggling to work and care for a toddler, she needed all her grit just to survive. Eventually she realized what was happening to her and left the hospital environment that was making her so sick. She became her own lab rat, slowly recovering as she identified and eliminated a variety of toxins from her life. That "death and rebirth" experience changed the way she practiced medicine. It was part of the long and almost mythical path to finding her purpose in life that she will write about in the books that follow.

I think about her journey to purpose as an ascent up a steep mountain, where at times it must have seemed like there were no footholds. The result—after months of grave suffering—was a deep gratitude for life.

A blog post she wrote about that experience ends with a picture of her, arms outstretched, and the caption "Still dancing."

Erica is the most joyful person I know.

Now, back to the story of our summer's walk. As our shadows grew longer in the fading daylight, we headed back to Erica's adobe home, made of the same red earth as the mountains that rose around us, intimate and nourishing.

We sat down to a simple dinner of delicious organic vegetables and locally raised lamb. Erica assured me that she had personally visited the sheep ranch where the lamb was raised to make sure that the animals have a good, natural life. She should know, since she was a sheepherder for several months when she lived among the Navajo.

We sat outside on the back porch and watched the sun go down as we ate our meal. After the dishes were cleared away and the stars appeared in the night sky, Erica decided that the first book in a series of four would tell the story of her time with the Navajo—first as a young teacher, and then as a doctor.

Now that you know a little about Erica, I'll say a few words about the incredible story that you are about to read. A memoir of courage and connection, *Medicine and Miracles in the High Desert* opens the door to a magical world filled with meaning, love, and insight. An antidote to the anxiety, separation, and polarization of our world today, Erica's story offers hope that with a will to serve and an open heart, miracles are possible.

I have heard most of the stories you're about to read from Erica's own lips. She is a riveting storyteller as well as a prodigious writer. You can read more of her stories, and access eminently helpful medical information, on her blog, *Musings, Memoir and Medicine*, www.musingsmemoirandmedicine.com.

When I first read her stories of teaching school on the Navajo reservation as a recent college grad, I thought of Parker Palmer, a globally renowned writer and speaker who addresses compelling issues in education and in the wider social fabric of community. Palmer teaches that in all sectors of life, success flows from creating personal connections that are "soul to soul," rather than "role to role."

Think about it. Why would Navajo children relate to stories about Dick and Jane written for a totally alien Anglo culture? Instead, Erica encouraged the children to write stories about events from their own lives. She visited their homes and learned to spin and dye wool, weave classic Navajo rugs, and herd sheep on horseback. She had the privilege of attending sacred ceremonies and learned the complex Navajo language, which was used as the foundation of an unbreakable code during WWII.

Erica's own soul was enriched as she honored the souls of the Navajo.

Spirituality, our deepest sense of meaning and connection, is the sturdy fiber from which Erica's stories of medicine and miracles are spun. Sometimes we need herbal or pharmaceutical medicine, a good ER, surgery, acupuncture, or a new diet to help us heal—but connection is the most powerful medicine of all. The thread of love that binds us together is the warp on which this memoir—as beautiful and intricate as any Navajo rug—is so skillfully woven.

And when you read the last sentence, the luscious taste of the stories still lingering in your mouth, rejoice. No need to grieve the loss of this wonder. There are more books yet to come.

ACKNOWLEDGMENTS

When I first shared the diary, photos, and cassette tapes documenting my time with the Navajo people, my friends and family urged me to turn this story into a book. I was so busy living my life that it took me over 40 years to act on their encouragement.

When I finally resolved to start writing, I went on a retreat with Natalie Goldberg. She is famous for helping budding writers get over their self-doubts and turn off their inner critic. I learned to internalize Natalie's unfiltered words to her students, "Shut up and write." I stopped making excuses and started writing.

I took two writing workshops with Anne Hillerman, daughter of Tony Hillerman, best known for his detective series involving two Navajo policemen. Anne gave me the inspiration to believe that I could turn my diaries into a book.

Still a bit intimidated by the idea of writing books, I started blogging as a way to slowly immerse myself into the world of writing. My blog posts are a mixture of medical topics and memoir. With a few revisions, some of the standalone memoir posts eventually became chapters in this book.

My friend John Kadlecek helped me to take the posts about my time with the Navajo people and turn them into a cohesive narrative.

My neighbor and editor, Kristin Barendsen, worked with me to copy edit the manuscript, catching typos as well as larger issues with her eagle eye. She stood by me as my ally, helping me make final content and design decisions.

My graphic artist friend Robert Railey converted my old color photos, taken with my little Instamatic camera, into sharp black-and-white prints, as required for printing. He also expertly created the book's beautiful cover with collaborative input from my friends and family.

Joan Borysenko's enthusiastic support encouraged me to keep writing. She made the process of finding a publisher less onerous by introducing my writing to her own agent, Patty Gift.

Patty led me toward Balboa Press, which has given its time and resources to turn this project into a book I can hold in my hands.

I am grateful to my sisters—Vreni Merriam, Jacqueline Paskow, and Veet Deha—for their many valuable suggestions. And to all the friends, family members, and patients who never gave up in their encouragement and support of my writing—a big, heartfelt thank you.

And thank you to my Navajo friends who read the manuscript and gave their thumbs up.

As you can see, a whole tribe of friends, family, and publishing professionals helped me take this book into the light of day.

INTRODUCTION

I went to the Navajo Reservation to teach school. What I received in return was one of the most impactful and transformative educational experiences of my life.

Upon my arrival, I was surely viewed as just one more white person in the stream of outsiders who came to the reservation to cheat and exploit the Navajo people—or to "help" by imposing their worldviews and ways. These outsiders included lawyers, government officials, developers, anthropologists, Mormons, Catholics, Presbyterians, and schoolteachers like me.

After my first discouraging week on the job, I made an earnest attempt to speak the Navajo language and understand the culture. From then on, my interactions changed dramatically. The kids in my classroom began to welcome me into their homes, their ceremonies, and their hearts. They introduced me to a world I never knew existed—a world that changed my life.

The BIA boarding schools were notorious for their cruel policies that stripped the Native children of their language, culture, and identities. Fortunately, the supervisors at Chinle Boarding School, where I taught, were surprisingly accepting of the Navajo children's heritage and did not object when they spoke in their own language.

While most of the teachers at the boarding school adhered closely to the standard curriculum, the principal allowed me to create my own curriculum without interfering. To this day, I don't know why he gave me such leeway. Perhaps he sensed that we were on the threshold of a nationwide movement toward bilingual education for non-English-speaking people. Toward the end of my first year of teaching, my classroom was chosen by the government to be part of its bilingual pilot program.

Thirteen years after I left the reservation, I returned to the Navajo people as a newly minted medical doctor. At the end of my two years of service in Cuba, New Mexico, I received a blessing that would powerfully affect me for the rest of my life. The gift came from one of my patients—a Road Man, or medicine man, who conducted peyote ceremonies.

Throughout this book, I have used the term *Navajo* because that's what people said back then, and I wanted to recreate the context of those times. Today, however, it's considered more accurate and respectful to use the term *Diné* when referring to "The People."

I changed the names of a few of the people to protect their privacy. And throughout this book, I have been careful not to reveal sensitive information about the ceremonies I participated in. I have withheld many of the details out of respect.

Erica Elliott
October 2018
Santa Fe, New Mexico

CHAPTER 1

The Dead Medicine Man

Cuba, New Mexico, 1986

It was early summer—monsoon season—when I began my first job as a medical doctor, fresh out of training in family practice. An overcast sky greeted me on the day of my arrival, along with thunder and lightning.

Overhead, a dark cloud released a curtain of rain that poured down hard against my car, driven by gusts of wind. Within minutes, the red clay road turned into slick mud. My two-wheel-drive Honda slid from one side of the road to another as I struggled up the long incline toward my new home in the foothills of the Jemez Mountains overlooking the little town of Cuba, located in a remote area of northern New Mexico.

A four-wheel-drive pickup truck sailed past me. The driver peered through the side window at me, no doubt wondering about the newcomer snaking around in the mud.

After I finally reached the two-room adobe house that I had rented sight unseen, I spent the next few hours hauling my belongings into the musty, mouse-infested building.

By the late afternoon, as the sun was low on the horizon, I decided to take a break and drive back down the road to town. I wanted to introduce myself to the doctor on duty and other staff members at the clinic.

I hopped back into my muddy car. The steep, slippery road meandered through spectacular scenery with otherworldly rock formations and towering ponderosa pine trees. The invigorating, crisp mountain air smelled delicious—even in the rain.

As the road rapidly descended, the landscape became more typical of the high desert—dotted with sagebrush and interspersed with piñon and juniper trees. Rabbits darted in and out of my peripheral vision as I concentrated on keeping my wheels outside the deeply carved ruts in the road.

Once I finally turned off the bumpy dirt road and reached the pavement, I spotted a series of long, low, ramshackle buildings made of partially rotted wood with tin roofs. The sign in front read "The Cuba Health Center." The building housed a nine-bed hospital along with a busy emergency room and outpatient clinic.

I tried to enter what looked like the front door but found it locked. I knocked on the door. No answer. I knocked louder and waited while the rain beat down on me. A Hispanic emergency medical technician in blue scrubs opened the door a crack, stuck his head out, and said, "What do you want?"

Taken aback, I responded warily, "I'm the new doctor." He looked me over briefly and then opened the door wide to let me in. He said, "We've been waiting for you." He had a mischievous smile on his face that I didn't know how to interpret.

The EMT led me to a small room where the medical practitioners wrote in their charts at the end of the day. Inside the room, the doctor on duty sat leaning back in his chair, with his feet on the desk. His piercing green eyes looked me over from head to toe in a friendly and flirtatious way. Then he took his feet off the desk, sat up in his chair, and said, "Hi, Erica. My name is Bill. You have no idea how glad we are to see you. I'm ready for a break from this place."

Bill had been trained in emergency medicine. The administration in Santa Fe hired him on a temporary basis to work at the clinic until a permanent doctor could be found—someone willing to serve time in this isolated stretch of the Southwest.

It was a few minutes past five o'clock. I asked Bill, "When do you get to go home and get some rest?"

His answer took me by surprise. "I'm going home right now. You're on call tonight. We'll be alternating nights on duty. It's just you and me, Doc. Tommy here will show you around," he said, gesturing to the EMT who had let me in. "He's one of our best EMTs. Good luck."

I could never have imagined what was waiting for me that night.

Before Tommy went off duty for the evening, he gave me a tour of the facility. We walked down the dark, poorly ventilated hallways, stopping intermittently for cursory introductions to the various staff members as they were leaving for the day. After the brief tour, Tommy turned to me and said matter-of-factly, "You'll be on night duty, starting now, until tomorrow morning. Then you'll be seeing patients in the clinic all day. Good luck."

I noted that both Tommy and Bill had ominously ended their sentences with "Good luck."

Tommy's casually dispensed news that my tour of duty was about to begin at that very moment made my mouth go dry and my heart race. Before my senses could register what was happening, the clinic began to pulse with action as patients came in after hours to be seen for their ailments.

On his way out the door, Tommy added that a Navajo medicine man had been run over repeatedly, with a vengeance, by a drunken acquaintance in a truck. The crime had happened in front of a bar about 30 miles away. The driver had been charged with attempted murder.

"Oh, I forgot to mention that the two EMTs we sent out to get him are stuck in the mud. One of them just radioed in and wants to know what he should do."

Not having a clue what the stuck EMTs should do, I asked Tommy how they would normally handle this situation. "Well, we would send out our other ambulance, but the battery is dead."

A third EMT managed to recharge the dead battery, then sped off into the last light of the sun. I bolted into the trauma room to make a quick study of where everything was located while I waited anxiously for their return. A kind nurse practitioner, fairly new to Cuba, stayed and helped me get set up.

As we were running back and forth from the supply room to the trauma room, I noticed something odd at the end of the long, unlit hall. Water was trickling in under the clinic's main entrance door. The stream of advancing water looked like a snake slithering sideways toward us, ever expanding in its width.

The nurse practitioner noticed the bewildered look on my face. "The maintenance man was supposed to fix that drainage problem today," she said, annoyed. "I guess he didn't get around to it. Whenever there's a big downpour lately, the water gets funneled right into the clinic." By the time she finished speaking, the water had reached my shoes and stopped just short of covering the tops.

4

The ambulance finally arrived back at the clinic. The EMTs carried the lifeless medicine man on a gurney into the tiny emergency room. He was not breathing and had no detectable blood pressure or pulse. He was DOA—dead on arrival.

Having only intubated anaesthetized dogs and plastic mannequins in my medical training, I took a few seconds to say a short, silent prayer, "God help me." I took a deep breath and charged forward.

Upon opening the patient's mouth to suction out the blood, I could see that the back of his throat was crushed. Intubation by the normal route would not be possible. I took another deep breath, grabbed a scalpel, and punctured a hole in the patient's neck below the thyroid gland in order to insert a breathing tube. As I pressed my finger on the incision to stop the bleeding, I yelled, "Where are the intubation tubes? Someone find me a tube." My voice rose in pitch. "I need it now." Someone let me know that the ER had recently run out of intubation supplies.

"Do you have a ballpoint pen?" I breathlessly addressed the EMT standing next to me. He nodded. "Give me your pen, but take the inside part out first. Hurry."

I pushed the empty barrel into the hole and blew into the makeshift tube. The ballpoint pen technique was something I had heard about from medics who had served in Vietnam. After I performed mouth-to-pen resuscitation for a few long minutes, the physician's assistant found an intubation tube in one of the drawers.

We replaced the ballpoint pen with the tube and then attached the oxygen supply. Those few minutes felt like an eternity.

The moment we completed the intubation, I allowed myself a nanosecond of amazement that I had just performed my first crycothyroidotomy on a real human being.

But the procedure did not do any good—given that the patient's heart had stopped beating before his body arrived at the clinic. One of the EMTs performed manual chest compressions with little success. It was time to try the defibrillator, electric paddles on the chest, to jolt the heart's electrical system into action.

With our feet in ever-rising water, it seemed like a good idea to move to another room to avoid electrocuting ourselves. We raced the gurney down the hall, looking for a room with a dry floor. We swung the gurney through the doorway into the supply room.

Although I had never used a defibrillator in my medical training, I knew where to place the paddles. I held my breath as I squeezed the paddles to activate them. The medicine man's body jumped and jerked on the gurney. After a couple of tries with the defibrillator, his heart began to beat erratically, without enough force to create a detectable blood pressure.

The EMT who drove the ambulance that had carried the medicine man back to the clinic did a chest x-ray with the patient supine on the gurney. The x-ray revealed that the medicine man's chest had been crushed, with all the ribs fractured, and blood had pooled in his lungs and chest cavity.

The medicine man needed to have a chest tube inserted to clear out the pooled blood. I wondered how doing the procedure on a human would compare with the ones we residents had been forced to perform on anaesthetized dogs during our medical training.

Most family practice residency programs do not train doctors for emergency room medicine. I had little choice but to do whatever I could to save this man's life, even though he was technically already dead.

I wondered if any of my classmates had experienced this level of trial by fire—unsupervised—on their first day of doctoring after graduation from residency training.

The nurse practitioner rummaged around and found the primitive, jerry-rigged glass jar with two tubes coming out of the stopper that the doctors at the Cuba Health Center used for draining blood and other secretions from the chest. With another wordless prayer, I pushed the scalpel into the precise spot between the ribs and inserted a tube that immediately reddened with escaping blood.

After one of the EMTs placed a catheter in the man's urethra to monitor urine output, there were no more procedures left for us to do. I could now stand back, breathe, and assess the situation.

The medicine man barely clung to life with a faint, erratic heartbeat. I was in way over my head and needed help. I had instantaneously gone from being a doctor-in-training to being a real doctor in the trenches, improvising on my own and using procedures that I had only read about in books or tried on plastic mannequins and helpless dogs. Fortunately, I had the support of experienced EMTs and nurses during that unforgettable evening.

At my request, one of the EMTs placed a call to the emergency department at the University of New Mexico in Albuquerque and relayed the dire situation to the doctor on duty. The ER doc immediately dispatched a trauma surgeon and crew by helicopter. Their estimated time of arrival: one hour.

By the time the helicopter landed, our resuscitation efforts had already ended after two hours of futile attempts. The EMTs notified the medicine man's family members of his death. Word spread rapidly throughout the community. His people had already started arriving at the clinic and were gathering in the waiting room even before we had pronounced the patient dead.

The trauma surgeon jumped out of the helicopter just as it landed on the little pad behind the clinic. He dashed toward the clinic ready to spring into action. I hung my head and said that the patient was dead, and related the whole story to the eager and highly caffeinated young doctor while I choked back my tears.

He put his hand on my shoulder and congratulated me for being able to get even a few heartbeats. He tried to comfort me by saying that only one percent of victims found "in the field" with a non-detectable blood pressure can be resuscitated. He took a brief look at the dead man with tubes in every orifice and then shook my hand and said with a sincere look on his face, "Good job. Keep up the good work."

He dashed back to the helicopter and took off. I darted into the bathroom and cried into a towel, muffling the sound of the sobs. I felt bowled over by all the tumultuous feelings that I had suppressed throughout the evening. After a few minutes, I reined in my emotions, rinsed my face with cold water and snapped back into action. The night was still young.

On my way to the waiting room to talk with the grieving family, one of the EMTs announced, "There's a pregnant Navajo woman with seizures on her way to the clinic."

In the meantime, all the chairs and standing areas in the waiting room had been filled with friends and relatives of the medicine man. At first, the Navajo people appeared angry that the medicine man had not been saved, probably without realizing the condition he had been in when the EMTs transported him to our little hospital. I assured them that we had done everything possible to save his shattered body. I handed one of the relatives a paper bag with the medicine man's turquoise necklace, silver bracelet, old turquoise earrings, and his headband, along with a few dollar bills that I'd found in his pockets.

I spoke from the heart, barely holding back the tears, in a combination of English and Navajo. Hearing the new doctor speak Navajo disarmed them. Their hostility dissipated before my eyes. Some even smiled with surprise. I expressed to them my heartfelt sorrow. When the Navajo people had no more questions for me to answer, I shook each person's hand as they filed past me. To the Navajos remaining in the room, I excused myself.

By then it was well past midnight. The next couple of hours I spent monitoring the pregnant Navajo woman, who was in the throes of potentially life-threatening seizures that were related to extremely high blood pressure—known as *eclampsia*. Her body convulsed repeatedly while her eyes rolled back in her head. I placed an IV in her arm and added magnesium sulfate to the intravenous solution, a mineral that is vital for stopping seizures. Magnesium relaxes the smooth muscles that line the blood vessels.

I sat with the stoic young woman, still dressed in her traditional clothing, until her blood pressure stabilized and the seizures stopped. An EMT wheeled her into the little nine-bed hospital, extending like a warehouse off the clinic, where the nurse on duty could monitor her.

A steady trickle of people came in throughout the night with problems less likely to raise my adrenaline levels, like sick babies with ear infections, a woman in false labor, a man with acute alcohol intoxication, and other more routine ailments. I felt relief wash over me because finally I could treat problems that I had been well trained to deal with.

When the Health Center finally quieted down that night, I decided to drive home to try to get a couple of hours of sleep.

But before I could get to the end of the hall, a young Hispanic woman came in moaning in labor. Her two sisters, mother, and grandmother accompanied her. I turned around and headed for the delivery room. The woman had received no prenatal care, which is not uncommon in isolated, rural areas.

The woman groaned and screamed from the pain, unlike Navajo women, who often labor silently. Her relatives gathered around her, holding her hand, stroking her head, and wiping her face with a cool washcloth.

9

Fortunately, the delivery went smoothly. As the family squealed with delight when the baby came out of the birth canal, I wiped away tears of joy with the back of my gloved hand. My first night shift as a neophyte doctor ended on a celebratory note.

The joy dissipated when I looked up at the clock and saw that it was already daytime. More patients would be streaming into the clinic in less than an hour. I had no time to go home and rest. No time even to shower or eat a real breakfast.

I walked out of the clinic into the sunlit morning after what had seemed like an interminable night shift taking care of a steady stream of emergencies. The rain had finally stopped. The air smelled clean and invigorating. I headed straight to the convenience store across the street and drugged myself with a sugary donut and washed it down with coffee so I could keep going after working all night.

A tall Navajo man walked over to the little table in the corner where I sat alone, eating my junk food breakfast. He said he wanted to talk to me. I recognized him; he had been in the room with the family members of the deceased medicine man. I braced myself for a barrage of criticism for not having saved his relative's life. Instead, he was polite and friendly. He asked me how I knew how to speak Navajo. I told him that long ago, when I was very young, I had been a schoolteacher on the reservation at Canyon de Chelly.

CHAPTER 2
Chinle, Arizona

Fall 1971

"Good morning, class. My name is Ms. Elliott," I announced cheerily as I stood in the front of the room and looked out over the rows of brown faces. No one looked at me. All eyes looked down in an almost studious effort to avoid my gaze. There wasn't a sound. I repeated my greeting in a louder voice, "Good morning, class. I'm your new fourth-grade teacher." I waited for a response. The room remained silent.

Trying to engage the students, I asked a string of questions. "What is your name?" I said, pointing to the boy in the second row near the aisle. When the boy did not respond, I looked at my seating chart, pointed again at the boy and said, "You're Billy Begay." He cringed as though I had shot him with a dart.

Refusing to give up, I asked the girl at the edge of the third row, "Where do you live?" She bent her head all the way forward onto her chest, her long black hair falling forward onto the desk, covering her face. Her silence and lack of eye contact threw me off balance.

Things went from bad to worse. One of the girls sitting in the first row, Evelyn Tsosie according to my chart, leaned over her desk and spit onto the linoleum floor. I stood in disbelief.

I decided it was time for some discipline and demanded that Evelyn clean up her spit. She made no response or acknowledgment that she had heard me. I insisted again in a louder, more authoritative voice. She remained silent and immobile, her head bent forward.

Flustered and red-faced, I was at a loss for what to do next. I finally cleaned up the spit myself. While crouching on the floor to clean up the brown-colored spit, I noticed that it contained chewing tobacco.

I knew that old cowboys use chewing tobacco, but a 12-year-old girl?

My first day of teaching left me shocked and confused. The teacher training I'd gotten at Antioch College had not prepared me for the cultural chasm that lay between me—the eager, young, inexperienced white woman—and the Navajo people. I had received no orientation—not even a manual—to help me navigate this unfamiliar territory.

Maybe I made a mistake accepting this job.

While finishing my last semester of college in the spring of 1970, I had skimmed through the trade journals for teachers in the college library. In one of them I saw an opening for a fourth-grade teacher at Chinle Boarding School on the Navajo Reservation in northern Arizona, operated by the Bureau of Indian Affairs (BIA). Without knowing why, I felt a strong magnetic pull to apply for this teaching position. I submitted my application to the BIA, but received no response.

In fact the BIA had responded, but the letter didn't reach me because I had been traveling in Europe and the United States since graduating from college. The letter was forwarded to several different addresses, but never arrived in time to find me still at those locations.

The well-traveled letter reached its final destination at my sister Vreni's home in Venice, California, toward the end of September 1971—more than a year after I had sent in my application.

Around that same time in September, while hitchhiking in the West with my dog, I paid a visit to Vreni. When I arrived, she handed me the life-changing letter.

The BIA had offered me the position that I had applied for. When I called the BIA office in Washington, I discovered to my surprise that the position had remained open during the entire past year without a single application other than mine.

Although the school year had already begun a month earlier, the principal at the boarding school wanted me to start immediately.

I hastily made preparations for my new life as a schoolteacher. My brother John in Seattle agreed to take care of my dog. Vreni lent me some of her clothes, since all I had was what fit in my backpack. She also lent me $700 so I could buy a cheap, maroon-colored Volkswagen van that I'd seen advertised in the local paper. The owner had turned the van into a camper with a bed in the back. He had spray-painted a huge, white peace symbol on one side. I felt proud of myself for having purchased my very first vehicle—even though it looked like a piece of junk.

I left behind the life I had known and headed off to the Southwest, having no idea about the world I would find there.

As I leisurely drove through spectacular landscapes with otherworldly rock formations on the way to the Navajo Reservation, I had to remind myself that I was still in the United States. I had never seen such a big sky. My spirits soared. I was 23 years old and about to begin my first real job.

The tiny town of Chinle, Arizona, lay in the middle of a vast, empty expanse of land, right at the mouth of Canyon de Chelly. One single paved road ran through town. The nearest city was Gallup, 120 miles away in the neighboring state of New Mexico.

When I drove up to the BIA school, housed in a long ramshackle one-story building, the principal came outside to greet me on the dusty playground. He was a black man from the South. In his neatly pressed suit and tie, he looked disapprovingly at my sandals, borrowed mini-skirt, and long hair, which looked disheveled from traveling all day with the windows rolled down. Then his gaze shifted to the hippie van with its huge peace sign on the side. A visible shadow of apprehension crossed his face.

Later, when the principal and I had become friends, he confessed to me over a few beers that when he first saw me, he feared that he had hired a young, wild, rebellious hippie who would not take the system seriously. I reassured him that I was not a hippie and never had been. I was merely unconventional.

I had my own apprehension and doubts about this place. I saw barely a blade of grass to offer relief to the eye from all the various shades of brown. The town itself seemed to be at least 20 to 50 years behind the rest of the world. The people drove pickup trucks and listened to coun-try-western music. The men dressed like cowboys. People seemed to know little about the world beyond the reservation.

And I, in turn, knew nothing about Navajo culture.

After a week of bewilderment due to my cross-cultural ignorance, I felt frustrated and forlorn. People in stores ignored me; my students still wouldn't speak to me. I understood that they probably viewed me like all the other white people who had come to the reservation to "help" them by trying to change their ways. And why shouldn't they?

I called my parents and told them I had made a mistake in my deci-sion to teach on the reservation—and I didn't want to continue in this strange and desolate place.

My father wisely suggested that I give the place a three-month trial before making a decision about leaving. He counseled me not to judge a place or people by first appearances.

I agreed to wait the three months, thinking I knew for sure what my decision would be.

But I resolved, in the meantime, to learn as much as I could about the Navajo people and their culture.

My teacher's aide, a Navajo woman named Donna Scott, had fully assimilated into white culture. When I shared with her my frustration with the students, she willingly agreed to help me understand what had transpired that first day in the classroom. She explained that the children did not respond to me out of deep shyness and had avoided my gaze as a gesture of respect.

I asked Donna why Billy Begay cringed when I pointed at him. She explained that traditional Navajos do not point their fingers at anyone or anything because pointing draws too much attention to the person or object and could be seen as a way of putting a hex on someone. Navajos point with their lips. Donna gave me a demonstration by puckering up her lips as though she were about to kiss someone. Through her puckered lips, she said *"Ńléidi,"* meaning "over there," as she looked off in the distance.

I noticed that everyone in the boarding school referred to one another using both their first and last name together. Donna Scott said that traditional Navajos do that to show respect. I tried to remember to use both names, but sometimes I forgot and just used the first name.

As for the spitting, Donna Scott explained that some of the children, like Evelyn Tsosie, come to class with a wad of chewing tobacco tucked inside their cheeks, making them bulge. They spit from time to time into wads of toilet paper while in class.

During their summer vacations, children return to their traditional homes, eight-sided log structures with dirt floors called *hogans*. Without running water or toilets or Kleenex, the people sometimes spat onto the dirt floor and then covered the spit with a little dirt from a flick of the foot.

That October, the children in my class had just returned to school—now that the school had a fourth-grade teacher—after spending four months at their remote homes in or around the surrounding canyons. Evelyn had simply made a mistake when she spat out of habit onto the linoleum floor. When I scolded Evelyn in front of the entire class, it caused her deep humiliation. To save face, she did not respond to me.

With Donna's help, I let go of my frustrations and found the humor in my displays of glaring ignorance that first week, as I stumbled around in a steady stream of cross-cultural mistakes and misunderstandings.

In addition to learning about the Navajo way of life, I made a commitment to learn the Navajo language. Donna taught me my first words to try out with the kids in the classroom. She tried to write out the words phonetically. That evening I practiced saying the difficult-to-pronounce words over and over until I had them memorized.

The Navajo language includes sounds I had never heard before in English or the European languages, like glottal stops, guttural sounds, clicking sounds, and the sound of air blowing while the front of the tongue is placed on the roof of the mouth. Every vowel has about six or more ways it can be pronounced, each of which changes the meaning of the word. I had to listen very carefully, because at that time, there were no English/Navajo textbooks or dictionaries I could refer to or study. I didn't know how to write phonetically the sounds I was hearing because of the lack of English equivalents.

The next morning I walked into the classroom and greeted the kids in Navajo.

"Yá'át'ééh sha' ałchíní. Shí éí Erica Elliott yinishyé. Nisha? Haash yinilyé?"

I said, "Hello my children. My name is Erica Elliott." I puckered my lips just as Donna had taught me and pointed them in the direction of Billy Begay and said, "And you? What is your name?"

The class erupted in gasps and giggles. The kids looked up at me with big smiles on their faces. Our eyes met for the first time.

From the moment when I first attempted to speak their language, the kids warmed up to me in a big way and took great interest in helping me learn new Navajo words. They found my pronunciation hilarious. I learned later that I often ended up saying something that did not at all resemble what I had intended to say, which caused squeals of delight.

From that day forward, I began falling in love with each of the 36 children in my fourth-grade class. I quickly learned their names and a little bit about their home life—how many brothers and sisters they had, how many sheep and horses their family had, what trading post they lived near, and most importantly, which clan they belonged to.

Clans are extended families. I noticed that one of the first things that traditional Navajo people say when they introduce themselves to another Navajo person is the clan they belong to, such as Black Water Clan, Big Medicine Clan, or Near-the-Mountain Clan. I found this far more poetic than the mundane way that white people identify ourselves, as where we come from and what we do for a living.

The children ranged in age from nine to 15, depending on how much time they had stayed out of school to help their families herd the sheep and tend to the younger children.

ERICA M. ELLIOTT, M.D.

My fourth-grade class in Chinle, Arizona, 1971

I was supposed to be teaching all the basic subjects normally taught in the fourth grade. In reality, each of the subjects turned into an English lesson since most of the kids struggled with the language and had difficulty forming complete sentences in English. For the first few months, I set aside the textbooks because the content had no relevance to their lives and was more suited to white, middle-class urban children. Surprisingly, the principal did not object when I deviated from the school's standard operating procedures.

Unlike the Navajo students who lived in town and went to the public schools, the boarding school students were away from their homes and families for nine months out of the year. Most of the children came from isolated areas, accessible only by four-wheel-drive vehicles or horseback.

Over time, as they began to trust me, I received many invitations from the children in my class to visit their homes and to observe and even participate in traditional Navajo ceremonies.

18

Within a few weeks, I realized that I needed a four-wheel-drive vehicle so I could explore the rugged landscape all around me. On a Saturday, I drove my rickety van to Albuquerque, five hours away, and traded it in for a green, four-wheel-drive Ford Bronco.

Nearly every weekend, I went through the bureaucratic paperwork that was required to check out a student from the dormitory. We would drive together in my Bronco to the student's family hogan, whether located deep in the recesses of Canyon de Chelly or on the surrounding mesas. Over the course of the school year, I drove every student in the class to his or her home at least once.

Most of the parents and grandparents spoke strictly Navajo in their hogans. I listened carefully so I could become familiar with the many different sounds and intonations.

Billy Begay was the first student who asked me to check him out for the weekend and take him home to his family in Canyon de Chelly. Billy was less shy than my other students, and he often had a smile on his face when he spoke to me. His family lived next to Spider Rock, home of the mythic Spider Woman, who taught the Navajo people how to weave. The tall red sandstone spire loomed hundreds of feet into the sky from the bottom of the canyon where Canyon del Muerto and Canyon de Chelly merge.

We left my Bronco at the rim of the canyon and hiked about three miles down a steep, narrow path to get to Billy's hogan.

Billy's family welcomed me with handshakes. The family sat around a long wooden table. The younger children stared at me in the dim light coming through a single small window. Billy's mother, with a barely visible smile on her face, motioned for me to sit down. She passed me a warm bottle of Coca-Cola and a plate of Jiffy peanut butter sandwiches made with Wonder Bread and made gestures for me to eat.

After a long stretch of awkward silence, I tried out a few phrases of Navajo that I had learned from my students, carefully mimicking the foreign sounds and inflections. My attempt to speak their language instantly broke the shyness barrier. Everyone in the family smiled with delight and surprise.

The family began making jokes with me, most of which I didn't understand. I saw how much they appreciated my efforts to learn about Navajo life.

After lunch, Billy beckoned me to join him outside. A makeshift horse corral stood next to the hogan. The horses acted jumpy, but we managed to get the rope bridles onto their heads and lead them out of the corral.

We spent the rest of the day outside with Billy's two brothers, racing our horses bareback on the bottom of the canyon. We clung to the backs of our horses, laughing and screeching with delight, free from all cares—a world away from the kind of restrained English-style horseback riding I did as a young girl at summer camp in New England.

A sudden cloudburst cut short our exuberance. Within seconds, little rivulets of water were flowing in braided channels down the canyon at a fast clip, a flash flood in the making. We galloped back to the hogan, jumped off our horses, and ran inside, soaking wet and shivering.

Before we had a chance to dry our clothes by the wood stove, we heard a piercing scream. Billy said it was Chee ("Red"), the horse I had ridden. We ran outside toward the screams and saw Chee stuck in quicksand halfway up his legs.

The river running through the canyon has patches of quicksand that appear after it rains, causing danger to vehicles and unsuspecting people and animals.

The chestnut horse snorted and flailed his head around. His eyes bulged with a look of terror. Billy grabbed a coiled rope hanging on the outside wall of the hogan. He lassoed the panicked horse and then tied the other end of the rope to the pickup truck. His father drove the truck forward an inch at a time, gently pulling the gelding out of the mud.

The exhausted but grateful horse nuzzled Billy and his father. Chee allowed me to throw my arms around his neck for a few seconds before he turned and galloped back to the corral.

We ended the day sitting around the wood stove, eating fry bread and mutton stew and telling stories, none of which I understood except for a word here and there. When they laughed, I laughed too—just because it felt good to join in on the laughter. The harder they laughed, the harder I laughed.

Night came quickly, making a return up the long, steep path risky. Billy's mother suggested that I stay the night in their hogan in one of their two metal army cots. I reluctantly agreed, feeling uncomfortable knowing that she would have to sleep bundled up in blankets on the floor, with sheepskins serving as mattresses, because I had taken her bed.

The next day in the early morning light, we hiked up the steep trail out of the canyon and drove back to the boarding school compound. I dropped Billy Begay off at his dormitory. He waved and gave me a big smile before turning and walking away.

The Monday following my weekend in Canyon de Chelly, I discovered that the entire class knew about my adventure with Billy Begay and his family. They quizzed me on every detail. Did I like the food? Did I eat the mutton stew and fry bread? Did I fall off the horse? Did I see any coyotes or rabbits?

Not wanting to waste an opportunity for teaching, I turned the experience into an English lesson. I gave each child a blank piece of paper and some colored pencils and assigned them the task of drawing a picture of the hogan, horse corral, and Spider Rock on the upper half of the paper. I asked them to write three sentences in English about their drawing on the lower half of the paper. Their writing ranged from one word to many words, from legible to illegible.

A boy who had remarkable artistic talent drew a picture of a horse racing in the arroyo. He drew a girl with a ponytail clinging to the horse's back, holding hunks of the horse's thick mane in each hand. Underneath the drawing, he wrote "MY TEECHIR."

Well before my father's suggested three-month trial was up, I had fallen in love with my students. And the land that had once looked dusty and desolate now seemed magical and enchanting.

I could never have imagined the life-changing transformation that I would undergo during my time with the Navajo people.

CHAPTER 3

Spirit Guide

Southern Utah, Spring 1972

The last manmade structure shrank to a black dot in my rearview mirror as I drove down the cracked, potholed highway without a car in sight. The unmarked turnoff to the left was barely visible between juniper trees and sagebrush, the place where the pavement turned to dirt. I had already explored this region of southern Utah once before during my time off from teaching, but this particular turnoff had escaped my attention.

Although I spent most of my weekends taking the students in my class to their remote homes in and around Canyon de Chelly, this weekend I had decided to return to Utah to explore the backcountry.

After I left the paved highway behind, the next 40 miles of deeply rutted tract led me into vast stretches of high-desert wilderness. Red rock slabs, towers, pinnacles, and cliffs soared into the cobalt blue sky. The crisp air smelled pungent with the essence of piñon pine and cedar.

I could tell from the faintness of the ruts that this stretch of road had not been traveled for a long time. I saw no other evidence of human activity. My Bronco kicked up clouds of rust-colored dust as I meandered along, daydreaming about my new life among the Navajo people.

I loved participating in Navajo culture and learning about how my students saw their world. The culture was earth-based with a strong relationship with nature. Animals were seen as kin and embodied special powers. They brought messages for the people they encountered.

As I was drifting deeper into these reflections, I saw something tan out of the corner of my eye. A medium-sized coyote with a long bushy tail darted in front of my slow-moving Bronco. In Navajo culture, when a coyote crosses your path, it means something big is about to happen. I couldn't remember if it was something big in a good way or something big in not a good way.

But then crimson red buttes and otherworldly geological formations started filling my windshield from both sides, pushing aside any concerns about the meaning of the coyote crossing my path.

Farther down the road, I suddenly remembered what one of the kids in my classroom had told me during our informal discussion about Navajo mythology. He said, "If Coyote crosses your path, turn back and do not continue your trip. If you keep traveling, something terrible will happen to you. You will get in an accident and be hurt or killed."

I thought about those words and wondered if I should turn around and go home. I decided that Navajo cultural beliefs didn't apply to me.

I was the only person around for miles and miles. Of course, if the car had broken down, I probably would have died from dehydration. But I was not thinking about practical matters. All my focus was on this magical place I had entered.

The rutted tract ended at a little spring. I kept driving a few more miles until I came to what looked like a sanctuary of rock formations, a perfect place to stop and explore.

Feeling certain that no one else was in the area, I took off my shoes and all my clothes, relishing the warm air caressing my skin. I climbed up the sandstone slabs with my bare feet, entranced by the red rocks, the enormous sky, the incense smell of cedar.

After scrambling around the rocks, exploring caves and crevices, I came upon a little pool of water, a catchment basin for the infrequent rains—a natural bath in the middle of the desert. I cupped my hands and splashed my face, soothed by the cool water. I slipped into the pool and pointed my face directly at the sun with eyes shut, still feeling the brightness streaming in.

After what seemed like a long moment outside of time, I lay down on a warm slab, spread-eagle on my back. All my senses were alive. I turned onto my belly and pressed my extended arms against the sandstone, crazed with love for the land—and grateful for this solitude.

When the sun went down, a chill quickly settled over the rocks. I put my clothes back on, but not the shoes. I wanted to continue feeling the rocks on my bare feet every moment. I hopped from one slab to the next, on a path that seemed to be laid out for me, keeping clear of the sharp spines of the cactus.

Having no flashlight, I wanted to be sure to find the perfect sleeping spot on a flat rock to spread out my pad and sleeping bag before it got dark. But it never got dark—the moon was full overhead, bright and electrifying.

I sat up in my sleeping bag and sang love songs to the moon until sleep overpowered me.

I dreamed that I was in one of the sheep and goat corrals belonging to the family of one of my students. We were in the corral looking for a sheep to butcher for a ceremony. There were a few goats, including a billy goat that smelled rank with the strong scent of musk that goats have during sexual maturity. We moved through them, trying to catch one of the sheep. The smell of the billy goat grew stronger and stronger.

The smell became so strong that it overpowered all my senses. When I felt my back on the hard rock, I realized that I was not in a corral, but in my sleeping bag and wide awake. Yet the smell of musk had followed me out of the dream and was still filling my nose. Before I could open my eyes, I heard a sniffing sound right next to me.

Without moving, I opened my eyes, and—*Oh My God, I am being sniffed by a mountain lion, inches from my face!*

His head was so close that I could see his black whiskers in the moonlight, the white fur around his mouth, and the tawny-colored hair on the rest of his face. I closed my eyes, frozen in fear, waiting for his claws to dig into my skin and tear me apart. Nothing happened.

Why doesn't he hurry up and eat me and get it over with?

I barely breathed while my heart pounded loudly in my chest. I stayed paralyzed for what felt like hours.

By the time I found the courage to open my eyes, it was daylight; the sun had already appeared on the horizon. Amazed that I was still alive, I looked around. There were no tracks visible on the sandstone rock. When I began stuffing my sleeping bag into its sack, the hair on my forearms stood straight up. The distinct scent of musk wafted up my nose—the only remaining evidence of the lion's presence.

I drove to the nearest town 40 miles down the road and, at a gas station, I told the attendant about my experience. He said, "Ma'am, you're one lucky gal to be alive. Them cats can rip you to shreds in no time. The reason that damn cat didn't kill you is cause you was too scared to move." The attendant said that if I had fought the mountain lion or tried to get away, I would have been killed for sure. "Cats go after things that move—that includes great big cats like the one you seen."

For months I remained obsessed with thoughts of mountain lions, seeking any information I could get from hunters, park rangers, biologists, and other people who had experienced close encounters with them. Mountain lions populated my dreams night after night for weeks. I awoke from these dreams with the feeling that the mountain lion was trying to communicate something to me that I didn't fully understand. When I drove to Gallup to go grocery shopping, I stopped at the library and checked out books about mountain lions. All the stories I read confirmed what the gas station attendant had told me. I knew it was true what the authorities said, but something was missing.

Why did that mountain lion sniff me up close—right next to my face? Is there another reason he didn't rip me apart and eat me? Am I still alive simply because I didn't move?

A few weeks after my encounter with the lion, one of the Navajo teacher aides at the boarding school invited me to visit her grandmother, who lived alone in a hogan deep in the canyon, tending her sheep.

We spent the afternoon sitting outside eating mutton stew and fry bread. My friend and her grandmother caught up with each other's news, which included the story of the mountain lion.

The old Navajo woman took a few puffs from her tiny hand-carved pipe as my friend told the story. Toward the end of the story, she looked at me with a toothless smile that lit up her ancient, deeply lined face. Her dark eyes were laughing. For the first time during the visit, she looked right into my face and spoke directly to me, no longer diverting her eyes in deference. My friend translated her words.

The old woman said I was "really lucky" the lion came to me. He was my spirit guide, she said. He came to give me his courage, strength, and intense focus because I would need those for what lay ahead. She said I would face many obstacles, some big and life-threatening—and, if I lived through them, I would have "a strong heart and powerful medicine to give to the people."

The three of us sat in silence as we watched the sun drop behind the canyon wall, followed by the fading light.

When I returned home that evening, I wrote down the old woman's words in my diary.

Over time, I forgot about those words.

CHAPTER 4

Medicine and Miracles in the High Desert

When I first began to speak in my broken Navajo, the rapport came instantaneously, accompanied by much laughter at my attempts at conversation. The more Navajo I learned, the more friendly and welcoming the people became. Many Navajos invited me to their homes to participate in ceremonies, some of which were normally closed to white people, like the peyote ceremonies where the participants used mind-altering plant "medicine" derived from a special cactus.

The peyote religion originated with the Plains Indians in the late 1800s and then spread to tribes throughout the country. This new religion became known as the *Native American Church*. Although peyote is classified as a controlled substance, the U.S. government permits Native Americans to use peyote, provided it is used in a spiritual context and not for recreation.

A young Navajo man who befriended me in a local café introduced me to the religion. Curtis Begay had just returned to the reservation after graduating from college in the Midwest. He told me that he looked forward to returning to his Native way of life and traditions. After we talked, he invited me to spend the weekend with his extended family at their homestead near the mountains.

I made it clear to Curtis that I wasn't looking for a boyfriend at that moment because I was enjoying my freedom as a single woman. He understood. Nevertheless, he and his family accepted me into their lives with open hearts, as though I were part of the family. The children addressed me as *Shadi*, meaning "my older sister." When they saw how earnestly I tried to learn the Navajo language and culture, they smiled with approval. One of the women confided in me that the family belonged to the Native American Church. In those days it was actually illegal for white people to attend peyote ceremonies.

Most Navajos rarely discussed their religious life with white people. When asked, they usually claimed they were Mormon or Catholic. It was not unusual for a Navajo to belong to two or three different religions at once. Each church offered certain benefits in its quest to save souls, like free lunches or secondhand clothing.

After I visited Curtis's family a few times, his mother invited me to participate in my first peyote ceremony. Her invitation filled me with great anticipation—along with a measure of fear, knowing that I was going to experience mind-altering plant medicine.

Curtis's mother asked me to call her *Shimá*, the Navajo word for "my mother." She said that her family had "adopted" me and I now had a Navajo family.

The women told me I needed to leave my white man's clothing behind, because I was going to enter into the Indian world for the sacred ceremony.

I took off my clothes and pulled out my traditional Navajo attire from the paper bag I had brought with me. The week before, I had made a light blue satin skirt and a dark blue velvet blouse with the sewing machine that I had bought in Gallup especially for this occasion. I wound a hand-woven red wool sash around my waist, then covered it with a large silver concho belt.

Turquoise hung from my pierced ears and circled my wrists. A silver squash blossom necklace adorned my neck, and deerskin moccasins covered my feet. Shimá wound my long hair into the traditional Navajo knot, worn by both men and women, called *tsiiyééł*. She wrapped the knot with white yarn.

My reflection in the dusty and cracked mirror looked positively regal. I felt like I was going on my first date, with the same nervous excitement.

Finally, late in the evening, we filed into a special hogan reserved for ceremonies and took our places in a big circle. We sat with our woolen Pendleton blankets on the hard-packed dirt floor. The strange new sights and smells put me into a dreamlike state of wonder.

A fire was burning in the middle of the hogan. The wood had been placed in a unique configuration, obviously of some significance. The incense-like odor of the burning piñon and juniper logs wafted up my nose, creating a mystical sensation.

The Road Man, the elder who led the peyote ceremony, sat on the west side of the hogan, facing the door on the east side. A crescent-shaped mud wall about three inches high stood in front of him. It looked like a low altar with a large peyote button centered on top.

The peyote had come from a place in southern Texas, near the border with Mexico, where the landowner had given the members of the Native American Church permission to harvest the fruit from the cactus once a year.

The Road Man, bedecked in turquoise, sat with his legs crossed and his back straight. He had a solemn expression on his face and spoke in a slow and measured cadence. I imagined that he was explaining the purpose of the ceremony. Shimá told me that this ceremony was for healing a baby who had been sick with a high fever for many days in spite of white man's medicine.

I could not understand anything that the Road Man said because my Navajo language skills at that point were still rudimentary at best.

On the other side of the circle from me, I saw the attentive mother holding the sick and listless baby, bundled up in a small Pendleton blanket and strapped to a cradleboard. His cheeks looked copper-colored from the fever.

The Road Man passed around the "medicine" in three forms—a powder, a tea, and a "button," the large bud from the cactus.

All the forms of peyote tasted revolting to me. I gagged, trying desperately not to vomit. Shimá had told me that when people vomit during the ceremony, it means that the evil within them is being expelled. I surely didn't want all these people to see the evil inside of me. So I managed to keep the peyote down in spite of a few dry heaves that I disguised as coughing attacks.

As the night progressed, the prayers became more impassioned. The people implored God and Jesus to help the sick baby, and to help all the sick Navajo people, especially the wounded Vietnam vets. I watched both men and women wipe away their tears.

The peyote meeting broke all stereotypes that white people might harbor about traditional Navajo people being passive, non-communicative, and without emotion.

At certain times during the ceremony, the Road Man passed around sacred tobacco, wrapped in carefully cut cornhusk squares. The tobacco came from plants gathered in the high regions of the sacred San Francisco Peaks north of Flagstaff, Arizona—before their gathering area had been turned into a ski resort.

As each person held the sacred cornhusk-wrapped tobacco, he or she said a prayer, punctuated by a puff of tobacco smoke exhaled into the air. In between the prayers, the people sang and chanted to the hypnotic beat of a water drum that sounded like the pulse of life, in sync with my own beating heart.

When the sacred tobacco made its way around the circle to me, my Navajo mother, seated next to me, leaned over and whispered in English, "You can pass it on." Instead, I held onto the tobacco, took a puff, exhaled, and began to pray—in Navajo.

In the middle of my prayer, it dawned on me that I had understood most of what the people had said during the past few hours of the ceremony. I immediately dismissed the observation and assumed I was in a dream—or else so intoxicated from the mind-altering peyote that I was having a major hallucination. I kept waiting to wake up.

When I finished my Navajo prayer, I took another puff and blew the smoke out into the room to mark the end of the prayer, and then I passed the sacred tobacco to the person on my left.

A few minutes later, the water drum came to the person seated on my right. I began singing one of the peyote songs—in Navajo—accompanied by the beating drum.

This fantastic dream feels more realistic than real life. I must be really high.

As the night moved into morning, the peyote began to wear off. I slowly awoke from my dreamlike state, no longer able to understand what people were saying. I looked over at the baby. He looked alert and peaceful, with normal color in his cheeks. He made little gurgling sounds as he gazed at his mother.

At daybreak, we all filed out through the single opening to the east, then knelt down and touched our foreheads to the ground. We blessed ourselves with our eagle-feathered fans, extending our arms toward the sun so the rays would enter our bodies and bring healing to any part that might be ailing.

We all walked in silence to a nearby house built of cinder blocks, where some of the women had stayed up most of the night preparing us a feast for breakfast. They had spread a large white sheet on the floor. On the sheet I saw pots of mutton stew, plates of Navajo fry bread, and bowls of canned peaches.

As I ate my mutton stew, the Road Man began to talk to me in Navajo. When I told him that I didn't speak Navajo and didn't understand what he was saying, everyone laughed uproariously.

Then the Road Man said in English, "You sure talked up a storm in Navajo last night." I felt chills up and down the back of my neck.

How is this possible? How could I say prayers and sing songs I never heard before—and in a language that is foreign to me? I wonder if I briefly tapped into a past life as a Navajo woman—even though I don't really believe in past lives.

I had no idea how to explain this mind-boggling, mystical experience. I felt confused and tired. I would never be able to share this experience with anyone, since it defied rational explanation. I did not want to be labeled delusional, or at best, a liar. So, for many years, this was my secret, along with several other experiences I had while living with the Navajo people.

After I returned home from the peyote ceremony on Sunday morning, I felt foggy-brained from the sleepless night and probably from traces of peyote left in my system. As I puttered around my little apartment, I heard a motorcycle approaching outside. I peeked around the shades to see who was there, hoping not to be seen, since I was in no condition to entertain visitors.

A young white man dressed in a black leather jacket and black leather pants dismounted from his big, black motorcycle and approached my front door. As he knocked, I locked the door without making a sound. I had no idea who this person was—other than possibly a member of the Hell's Angels.

He kept knocking insistently. I waited apprehensively inside.

The young man walked around the side of the house, trying to peer in the window while I ducked out of view inside a hallway, feeling increasing fear.

The man went to the kitchen window at the back of the apartment and began to force it open and crawl inside. I took a deep breath, gathered my courage and marched into the kitchen, ready for a possible assault.

When the intruder—now inside my kitchen—saw my face, he beamed and said, "Hi Rickie. I didn't think you were home." Now I was totally confused. Only members of my family used the name "Rickie," a nickname from childhood.

I tried to act like I knew the man, as I stalled for time. "Where are you coming from on your motorcycle?" I asked, searching for clues to his identity. "Seattle. Aunt Judy said to send you her love." In that instant, I had a flash of recognition.

"John? Are you my brother John?" I hadn't seen my 20-year-old brother in several years. He had taken time off to explore the world. He was at an age where each year brought dramatic changes in appearance. We had a good, long laugh.

John stayed with me for a couple of days before moving on. I confessed to him that I might not have recognized him right away because I had just come back from being in another world. He expressed great interest in hearing about the peyote ceremony and wanted to know all the details. I didn't dare tell him the part about being able to speak and understand Navajo perfectly—and even sing and pray in Navajo— while on the peyote. I feared he would think I'd made the story up.

The peyote ceremonies continued to be a source of wonder and amazement that blew my concept of reality to smithereens. Each ceremony offered inexplicable experiences for me to ponder during the ensuing years.

On one occasion, a group of Navajo people organized a peyote meeting to pray for rain. One of my Navajo friends invited me to participate in that ceremony.

The reservation suffered a major drought that year, 1972. Crops and livestock were dying. Washington declared the Navajo Reservation a national disaster area and sent helicopters to drop bales of hay for the livestock.

The ceremony took place in a teepee. Native American Church members held ceremonies in teepees during the warm months and in their traditional hogans during the colder months.

Dressed in my ceremonial regalia, I silently filed into the teepee with the others and took my place in the circle. The people prayed fervently. In addition to focusing on the drought, the prayers included a plea for the end of the war in Vietnam and a return of their warriors.

About an hour into the ceremony, I heard a light pitter-patter sound on the canvas of the teepee. The sound closely resembled that of rain. I dismissed the idea as being unlikely.

Midway through the ceremony, we had our customary break for anyone needing to pee. As I squatted in the night a few yards away from the teepee, I placed the palm of my hand on the ground. The earth felt damp. I assumed the dampness was just an illusion created by the peyote.

When daybreak came and I stepped out of the teepee, I noticed tiny desert wildflowers around the teepee. At breakfast, the women who had been up all night cooking commented on the fact that it had rained briefly during the night, but only over the teepee. After breakfast, I returned to see the little wildflowers. They had disappeared.

A friend took this photo with my Instamatic camera just before a peyote ceremony. I'm standing on the right with the grandmothers.

I participated in many ceremonies on weekends. Some of the ceremonies I remember vividly, including the sounds and smells, as though they happened yesterday. Of others, I remember only small fragments.

One scene I recall is of a man who burst into the hogan where we were praying. He said that there was some evil witchcraft taking place nearby and asked if the Road Man could come and help right away. The Road Man asked his assistant to take over while he investigated the matter. I never heard what happened with the witchcraft. No one wanted to talk about it.

Another noteworthy moment I remember vividly is the time when it appeared as if the participants could read my thoughts.

As I was looking at a turquoise ring I wore on the fourth finger of my left hand, it suddenly morphed into a wedding ring. I felt a wave of panic come over me at the idea that I might be married and not know it.

When I looked up, the Road Man was looking directly at my face and laughing. I looked around at the other faces in the room. Everyone was looking at me and smiling. I thought to myself, *This is so strange—no one will believe me when I tell about these ceremonies.* At that very moment, the Road Man said out loud, "No, they won't believe you. But you don't need to tell them about what happens here."

Geez. They know my thoughts! How is that possible?

During my second year on the reservation, my Navajo family arranged a peyote ceremony as a gift for my own healing. I had developed an enlarged lymph node under my jaw on the right side. Although I had no explanation for the enlarged node, I didn't feel too concerned.

Over the next few months, the lymph node continued to enlarge and became hard, but painless. I knew very little about medicine, but I sensed this might be something serious. Although by this time I felt scared, I tried to ignore it, hoping it would go away.

Eventually the lymph node got so large that one of my students asked me if I had a goiter. Her words woke me up and made me realize I had to do something right away. I took a day off from school and drove to the nearest health facility, a mission hospital nearly an hour away in Ganado.

Hospitals intimidated me. They had an unpleasant odor to them and tended to be places where bad things could happen.

A young internist in a crisp white coat saw me in his office. He looked alarmed after he palpated the mass. He said, "It's very hard and immobile. Not a good sign. It could be cancer." He wanted me to get the mass biopsied that same day. He said he would call me for the follow-up appointment as soon as the pathology report was available.

I escaped from the hospital without getting the biopsy, feeling panicked.

The next day at school I told my teacher's aide, Donna Scott, what had happened at the hospital. I confessed to being afraid. She said she knew a Hopi medicine man who might be able to help me.

That weekend I drove to the Hopi reservation to look for the medicine man. He was hard to find. I asked several people to help me. I finally found him herding sheep. He listened to my story. After looking at the lump, he said that his specialty did not lie in this area. He referred me back to a Navajo medicine man.

I tracked down the Navajo medicine man with great difficulty. The instructions involved turning right at a large sagebrush, then going over the wash and down the dirt road a ways until coming to two juniper trees. "Then go left until you see a hogan. Take the road on the right. Keep going over two more washes and then the road will disappear. Get out and walk down the sandstone ledges to the hogan where the medicine man lives."

After getting lost a few times, I finally found the medicine man. Like the Hopi medicine man, he told me that my lump was not his area of expertise. I felt dismayed.

When my Navajo family heard my story, they told me they knew a certain Road Man who could cure this problem. They generously offered to host the ceremony. They agreed to share the costs with another family who had a gravely sick baby who needed some special prayers.

Peyote ceremonies cost a lot of money to host. They required a sheep to butcher and the purchase of enough food to feed all the participants and their families. The Road Man charged relatively high fees as well. My Navajo family's generous offer deeply moved me.

During the ceremony, I got so involved in the praying and chanting that I somehow forgot about my lymph node. I concentrated heavily on the healing of the sick baby.

At daybreak, as we ate our breakfast on the floor of the cinderblock house, I noticed that every single person had their eyes fixated on me in an expectant manner. I didn't know what was happening. I felt awkward and self-conscious. Suddenly I remembered my lymph node. My hand flew up to my neck. The lymph node had disappeared.

Oh my god. I'm healed. No one will ever believe me in the outside world. This will be my secret.

CHAPTER 5

A Walk Through Time

Ever since I had arrived on the Navajo Reservation to teach at the boarding school, I roamed around Canyon de Chelly at every opportunity. Usually I traveled with my Navajo friends in a truck or on horseback.

One Sunday, in the pre-dawn hours of the morning, I went into the canyon alone, on foot. The air was clean and delicious, with a hint of sage and juniper. I could never have guessed what awaited me.

The mouth of the canyon opened wide to a wet, sandy bottom. Imprints of horses' hooves mingled with the tracks of truck tires and a faint set of ruts from wagon wheels, evidence of the comings and goings of life in the canyon. I couldn't resist taking off my shoes and adding my own set of tracks to the others. The cool, wet sand and water seeped between my toes.

The canyon started to come alive with shapes and colors as the light of dawn crept over the bottomland. As I walked, I sang a simple Navajo prayer song, an expression of my gratitude to be alive and a witness to the timeless landscape of ancient red rock formations all around me.

Canyon de Chelly

A wooden, horse-drawn wagon with rubber tires silently rolled past me, heading in the opposite direction toward town. Young children in the back of the wagon stared at me as they passed. They sat on stacks of large gunnysacks. I suspected that they were going to Garcia's Trading Post at the mouth of the canyon to sell their hand-woven Navajo rugs.

My Navajo friends taught me everything I knew about the canyon, including how it got its name. The Navajo word for canyon is *tsegi* (TSAY-ih), meaning "inside the rock."

When Spanish soldiers intruded into this hidden Navajo enclave—the first non-Indians to enter the canyon—they asked the name of the place that they had stumbled upon. The foreign sound of the word, *tsegi*, morphed in the mouths of the Spaniards into "chayee." The spelling eventually became Canyon de Chelly, or "Canyon of Canyon."

It is indeed the canyon of all canyons.

The canyon was first inhabited over 2,000 years ago by people who built their homes high in the cliffs by enclosing natural caves with stacked rocks and leaving spaces for doorways and windows in the rock walls. The location of their dwellings high in the steep walls provided safety from enemies and predators. The fertile ground below gave them rich farmland.

The Navajos refer to these people as the *Anasazi*—the Ancient Enemies. Considered to be the first Pueblo people, the Anasazi lived in this region for over 13 centuries. And then they disappeared. Today, Pueblo people prefer the term *Ancestral Puebloans* to describe their ancestors.

White House Ruins in Canyon de Chelly

My Navajo friends told me that a prolonged drought drove the Anasazi to the Rio Grande River, where they became the Pueblo people. Years later, a few of them drifted back and taught the Navajo people—the new occupants of the canyon—how to grow corn, beans, melons, and squash.

Navajo life in the canyon went uninterrupted for generations until one fateful day in 1863, when the people heard the thundering and pounding of horses splashing through the water, carrying U.S. Army soldiers led by Kit Carson.

The mounted brigade burned down hogans, destroyed crops and peach orchards, killed the sheep, and left the people without a source of food.

Soon after the attack, the soldiers rounded up every Navajo they could find and marched them to Fort Sumner, an army fort in the center of a million-acre reservation known as *Bosque Redondo*, a desolate place in central New Mexico.

Hundreds of captives died from cold and starvation on the forced death march. Soldiers shot the sick and raped the women. They kidnapped some of the younger captives and used them as slaves. Navajos refer to this tragedy as the *Long Walk,* a walk that took them far away from their beloved canyon.

It wasn't until five years later, in 1868, that the Navajo leader Barboncito and the U.S. government signed a treaty that allowed the remaining survivors to walk the 400 miles back home and rebuild their shattered lives.

As I wandered aimlessly through the canyon, I saw countless flowering desert plants, beautiful antidotes to my painful thoughts about the Navajo people's suffering.

A cluster of plants with bright yellow flowers caught my eye for their stunning contrast to the red earth around them. These shrubby evening primrose plants grew close to the ground. Each plant had four large petals that lay wide open, greeting the new day. As the sun climbed in the sky, the petals closed. Traditional Navajos used the evening primrose flowers as medicine in some of their ceremonies.

Not far away, bright yellow petals of the sego lily looked like a set of wide-opened mouths, singing the song of life with all their strength.

These foot-high plants grow from a bulb that the Navajos dug up and ate raw in former times.

At the bottom of a towering cliff in front of me, yucca plants—with their circular array of tough, sword-shaped leaves—looked like sentinels with bayonets standing guard over the beautiful, bulbous white blossoms that hung from the tall stalk in the center of each plant.

On our field trips into the canyon, the kids in my class showed me how their people made soap from the yucca root that they used for cleansing in traditional ceremonies. They told me the Anasazi made sandals out of the yucca fibers.

My meanderings through the canyon brought me to a grove of cottonwood trees growing a few feet from the water. I felt an urge to lie in the shade of their branches. Although it was still early in the morning and I wasn't yet in need of shade, I accepted the hospitality the trees offered.

As I lay on the ground, I felt the calming embrace of the earth and the stillness in the air. In the profound quiet, I heard a soft ringing in my head, a vibration—like the vibration of life itself.

I pulled out my diary from my backpack, but then placed it on the ground next to me, not wanting to miss a second of the life flowing around me.

The bubble of almost complete silence suddenly broke open, as the earth began to vibrate with the rhythmic thundering of horses' hooves and sounds of splashing water.

Were these sounds similar to what the people heard when Kit Carson and his soldiers came charging through the canyon?

Canyon de Chelly is a favorite hangout for wild horses whose ancestors date back to the Spanish invaders. They have no brands on their hides and no riders on their backs. They roam freely and belong to no one.

The air filled with their smells, snorts, and whinnies. The canyon came alive with their wild energy and seemed to shout out in celebration. They ran in my direction along the edge of the water, coming ever closer. My heart raced as I imagined the horses galloping right over me, trampling me into the sand. But the horses stopped abruptly a few yards in front of where I lay motionless and barely breathing.

Although I had an unobstructed view of them, they appeared to neither see me nor smell me. As slowly and quietly as I could, I rose to a sitting position and marveled at the primordial scene before me, one that was both terrifying and magnificent.

A buckskin stallion with a black mane and tail began making a ruckus with his snorting. He stomped his hooves and scraped his right front hoof repeatedly in the sand while his head bobbed up and down.

He raised his massive male body into the air, his penis fully revealed outside its sheath. He fell onto the back of one of the mares. The white mare screamed out during the mating. Her screams reverberated throughout the canyon, bouncing off the steep sandstone walls.

The stallion dismounted the mare, and as quickly as it had arrived, the herd of horses galloped away, heading up the river.

Stunned, I replayed the scene over in my mind as I sat spellbound under the cottonwood trees.

I looked up at the massive red walls that towered over me and bore silent witness to the life that flowed inside the canyon. I felt like a mere speck in this timeless tapestry—a grateful speck.

During those times, in the early 1970s, non-Navajos like me could wander freely in Canyon de Chelly and Canyon del Muerto without a guide. On the weekends, I spent entire days exploring the many side canyons, either on foot or horseback. The red rocks exuded magic and mystery. I couldn't resist climbing up into the caves that were accessible by slopes of talus and partially eroded toeholds that had been carved out of the rock hundreds of years before.

One day I explored a cave that was located halfway up the canyon wall and difficult to reach, with only precarious Anasazi toeholds for support. I leaned into the sandstone wall as I inched my way up to the cave and then climbed inside. Once my eyes adjusted to the darkness, I spotted a large pile of rocks that had obviously been placed there by someone. I had a strong feeling that something lay hidden under those rocks.

One by one, I removed the rocks from the pile. At the bottom of the pile I saw a small skeleton—probably an Anasazi woman from pre-Navajo times. Around her cervical spine lay a necklace made of small, irregularly shaped turquoise beads. Next to her stood a light-brown clay pot and a pair of disintegrating, grey-colored sandals woven out of yucca fibers.

Since the Anasazi had abandoned Canyon de Chelly by 1200 AD, I figured that the skeleton and the artifacts I uncovered in the cave must have been around 800 years old.

After staring at the sacred objects, I said a quick prayer for the spirit of the Anasazi woman, and then I carefully put the rocks back into a pile to cover the treasures and leave them just as I had found them.

I prepared for my descent to the floor of the canyon by squatting down on all fours. Turning to face the wall, I painstakingly lowered my body down from the edge of the cave. Images of Anasazi people climbing up and down the steep walls filled my mind.

The next day in the classroom, I proudly told the students about my find, describing in vivid detail what I saw. They responded with agitation and shock. They said I had done a very bad thing by disturbing their ancestors. I protested that I had not taken anything. They advised me to have a purification ceremony so that bad luck would not strike me down.

Donna Scott took me aside and explained that in Navajo religious belief, an evil spirit or ghost, called *ch'indi,* lingers around the dead person's bones and possessions. The ghost represents everything that had been bad in the dead person.

Traditional Navajos believe that contact with *ch'indi* can cause a severe, unexplained illness called "ghost sickness," which can lead to death if left untreated by a medicine man.

Seeing how upset the students became when I told them about finding the Anasazi skeleton in the cave, I agreed to consult with a medicine man if I developed any signs or symptoms of ghost sickness, like an unexplained serious illness or some exceptionally bad luck.

Given the amount of energy that the children had for the subject of *ch'indi,* I devoted the rest of the afternoon to letting the students teach me about werewolves, skin walkers, and shape shifters.

Ch'indi are shape shifters, like werewolves and skin walkers—terms that are often used interchangeably. All shape shifters are able to morph from humans to animals, and they can inhabit any living thing, including wolves, foxes, coyotes and owls. The kids told me that if I ever saw a wolf or coyote that walked upright like a human, then I could be sure it was a werewolf capable of great harm.

I asked how Navajos become werewolves. One of the boys explained that a man has to commit the worst crime possible in the Navajo culture—murder of a relative. After the murder, the man has the option of choosing a life dedicated to evil.

The students firmly believed in werewolves and witchcraft. Nearly everyone in class had a story about coming home and seeing a werewolf lurking around their hogan.

I was dubious, yet they spoke so convincingly of their own personal encounters with these entities that it made me take these paranormal accounts seriously. I asked the students if I needed to worry about werewolves coming around my ground-floor apartment in the government housing area. One of the students said that the skin walkers were not interested in *bilagáana* (white people), but that I had better stay out of their way or else I could get hurt.

After I dismissed the class at the end of the day, a student came to my desk and whispered in my ear that a certain Mr. Begay, a school employee, was known to be a werewolf. From then on, I always felt slightly peculiar when I saw Mr. Begay, imagining him racing around at night half-naked, with a skin on his back, doing evil deeds.

A few weeks later, I had an experience in Canyon de Chelly that made me question my disbelief in werewolves and witchcraft.

One evening on a school night, three young white women came over to my apartment and asked if I would take them into the canyon. They were student teachers from Utah who had spent the last month visiting the public high school in Chinle. Although I had previously agreed to take them, we had not set a date. I protested that their unanticipated visit was too late, especially on a school night. I remembered that my students had earnestly warned me to never walk around the canyon at night because that's when the skin walkers committed their evil acts.

The young student teachers pleaded with me, saying it was their last day on the reservation and that it was a perfect night since the moon was full. I reluctantly agreed.

We piled into my Bronco and drove to one of the trailheads. The light of the moon fully illuminated the canyon. The night was very still, interrupted only by the noisy chatter of the young teachers as we walked down the long trail deep into the canyon.

Halfway down, a flicker of light caught my eye. Across the canyon, I spotted a campfire burning in a cave near the top of a steep sandstone wall. I pointed out the fire to the student teachers. They were not impressed, saying that probably some hiker had camped up in the cave and made the fire to stay warm.

No, this was no camper, I countered. First, the Navajo people did not allow camping in the canyon by non-Navajos, I explained. Second, a hiker would need technical climbing gear in order to get up the nearly vertical sandstone wall. On that particular wall, the steps carved into the rock by the Anasazi people around one thousand years ago had eroded beyond use.

The sight puzzled me. The girls continued down the trail, oblivious of my concern. A few minutes later, I saw shadows projected onto the back wall of the cave. The elongated, distorted shadows moved rhythmically—the same movement and rhythm I had seen in ceremonial dancing.

The girls stopped and watched, finally beginning to sense that something strange and foreboding was taking place in the cave.

We sat on a rock, watching in silence across the canyon. At one point we heard a high-pitched whistle, identical to a sound I had heard in certain ceremonies. I knew that the whistle was made from the bone of an eagle's leg. The shrill sound pierced the night.

Immediately after we heard the whistle, the campfire went out. The canyon had an eerie stillness to it. Just as I was about to whisper that we should turn around and go home, a great clamor of barking and stampeding sheep echoed in the night.

Up the canyon a short distance from the cave, an old woman lived with her sheep and goats. It sounded like an animal was attacking her livestock. The melee lasted for about ten minutes, and then silence returned to the canyon.

While we sat watching the canyon below, I spotted a large animal loping along the floor of the canyon. It was smaller than a horse and larger than a dog. I thought it looked like a naked man bent over with a skin thrown over his body.

When I pointed out the figure to the young women, they jumped up and fled up the trail at full speed, finally realizing that something terribly bizarre and threatening was afoot below.

As I sprinted up the trail, I reminded myself that I was a *bilagáana* and, according to my students, werewolves and skin walkers aren't interested in white people. But they also said that if white people get in the way of werewolves, they could be harmed.

Relieved to reach the rim of the canyon, I jumped into my car and drove the student teachers to the dormitory, where I dropped them off. They got to have a truly paranormal Navajo experience, something they could think about for a very long time.

When I arrived home, it was way past my bedtime, but I was too excited to fall asleep. I got back into my car and drove to the trailer compound that housed the public high school teachers, one of whom I had befriended.

Seeing that Pat's light was still on, I knocked on his door. He had been grading papers. I told him the story. Pat laughed in disbelief and said I had a good imagination.

I challenged him to come to the canyon and see for himself, even though it was late. He accepted. I felt afraid, but my need to prove the truth of my story won out over my fear.

We reached the trailhead around midnight. The moon drifted in and out of the clouds, casting frightening shadows along the trail. My body stiffened with apprehension as we hiked down into the canyon. Neither of us said a word. At the bottom, we crossed dried-up cornfields and the arroyo, then more cornfields, until we reached the other side of the canyon.

We stood at the base of the sandstone wall, looking up at the cave, now dark and silent. A large talus slope made up of fallen rocks extended halfway up to the cave. Pat announced that he was going to climb as far as he could get. I stood at the bottom, excited and fearful, constantly looking over my shoulder for anything or anybody that might be stalking us.

As Pat scrambled up the talus slope, the loose rocks slipped beneath his feet, making loud noises that echoed like gunfire.

Halfway up, Pat heard a noise in the cave that startled him, nearly throwing him off balance. "Did you hear that? It must be a mountain lion," he said breathlessly. "There are no mountain lions around here," I said emphatically, as I positioned my body for flight in the opposite direction.

Just as Pat turned to continue scrambling up the talus slope, a snarling voice boomed out from the dark cave, "Get the fuck out of here, White Boy."

Pat nearly flew off the talus slope, stumbling and falling repeatedly on the way down. We both bolted out of there, propelled by terror. I ran with my back slightly arched, feeling as if someone was about to grab me from behind.

Once we had reached my car and were safely driving down the road toward home, I chuckled to myself. My credibility had been restored.

CHAPTER 6

Bilingual and Bicultural Education

Most of the teachers who worked for the BIA regarded me as an enigma in my enthusiastic embrace of life on the reservation. The majority of them were middle-aged white people who were looking forward to retiring from the government and moving back home.

In contrast to my colleagues, by my second year I had become so immersed in Navajo culture that I gradually found myself identifying with the Navajo people. Every couple of weeks when I left the reservation to buy groceries in Gallup, it struck me how sickly white people appeared, with their anemic-looking faces, as they pushed their grocery carts down the aisles. I had to remind myself that I was white just like those people.

During the school year, one of the books that I read in the evenings before going to bed was Dee Brown's *Bury My Heart at Wounded Knee*. When I read the part about the bloody massacre of innocent Native women and children and other atrocities committed by the Seventh

Cavalry in 1890, I hurled the book across my one-room apartment, furious at the American army for what they had done to "my people."

I kept forgetting that I was not a Native and that I came from a long lineage of northern European people. When my activist friends complained about white people, I found myself wholeheartedly agreeing with their observations.

Some of my Navajo friends nicknamed me *Adzán L'Chii*. They said that the name meant *Navajo Woman with Red Skin*—referring to my sunburned cheeks. I felt so closely identified with the Navajo people, I often felt like I was indeed a Navajo woman, especially during the ceremonies, when I dressed in traditional clothing and used my rapidly growing vocabulary of Navajo words and phrases.

Since the Navajo parents and grandparents of the children in my class spoke exclusively Navajo in their homes, I had a good opportunity to learn their language—by far the most difficult and complex language I had attempted to learn. In fact, the secret language system spoken by the highly decorated Navajo code talkers during World War II remains the only oral military code that has never been broken. The indecipherable "code" was simply the Navajo language used creatively.

I had some major challenges breaking the code, myself. Navajo is a tonal language, much like Chinese. If your voice goes up or down at the wrong place, or if the sound is cut off too soon, or not soon enough, you will say something you did not intend to say.

In my eagerness to delve into the intricacies of the language, I caused myself considerable embarrassment. The most distressing mistake I made involved a shy young boy in my class who had trouble with some of the writing exercises.

I had learned that it was best to help students privately in order to avoid humiliating them in front of their classmates. I asked the boy to stay after class so I could help him. In my attempt to make him feel more comfortable with me, I spoke to him in Navajo and said, "Come here, my relative," knowing that terms of kinship are used to express affection among the Navajo people. I said—or thought I said, *"Hágo shik'éi."*

The boy looked up at me in horror and ran out of the room. The next day he did not show up for class. I asked Donna Scott why he got so upset. When I told her what I had said, she gasped and put her hand over her mouth. "Don't ever say that. You told that boy to come and have sex with you."

Apparently my voice did not rise or fall in the correct way when pronouncing the "e," giving the word an entirely different meaning.

I stopped my attempts at speaking Navajo for a few days and gave a formal apology to the terrified boy, who forever after avoided eye contact with me.

I took my class on many field trips to places in our surrounding area. We hiked in the canyon and made trips to the grocery store, post office, and police station. After each trip, we would return to the classroom and the students would write about what they had experienced. Learning became exciting and meaningful for them.

The students knew how much I cared about them. The feelings were mutual, which made the teaching and learning process easy and fun.

I called the students *sha' áałchíní,* "my children." I addressed each boy as *shiyáázh,* "my son," and each girl as *shich'é'é,* "my daughter."

The principal told my students to call me Miss Elliott. The students shortened the two words to an affectionate "Elliott," pronounced as though it were two syllables, made with a staccato sound, "Ellit."

My parents came to visit me over the Christmas holidays my first year of teaching. They had heard my stories and wanted to meet the children.

Although Christmas did not have much meaning for most of the kids in my class, they had learned about the expression "Merry Christmas" from their former teachers. There is no translation in Navajo for the word "merry." And since the word "Christmas" contains sounds that were foreign to the students, they said it more like "Keshmish." With their eyes looking down, they shyly greeted my parents in Navajo, saying, *"Ya'at'eeh Keshmish,"* meaning "Good Christmas."

After the kids had recovered from the novelty of meeting my parents, they could barely remain in their seats. I had hung lemons, limes, and tangerines on the little Christmas tree in the back of the classroom. I chose those special treats for the children because they rarely had fresh fruit in their diets.

They excitedly waved their hands, yelling "Ellit, lemon!" or "Ellit, orange!" There was such a frenzied scramble for the fruit that I had to ask the students to get into a line and approach the tree one person at a time.

In 1971, the year I came to Chinle, the government implemented a prototypical program throughout the country for bilingual education in schools that served children whose first language was not English. The concept of bilingual education was a novelty in that era.

I had heard that until the change in policy, some boarding schools off the reservation were known to use extreme measures—including washing out the children's mouths with soap—as consequences for speaking Navajo while at school. These punishments were especially cruel given the fact that some of the kids hardly spoke English at all due to prolonged absences from school while helping out their families with childcare or herding sheep.

One day a film crew from the BBC, the British Broadcasting Company, came to my classroom to film bilingual lessons in action on the Navajo Reservation. Although the BBC was a British company, they sent a French team to make the documentary.

We sang songs for the film crew in Navajo and proceeded with our usual class activities, after which I spoke to the camera in French while the children giggled. I think they felt proud to tell the world about themselves.

The word spread all the way to the BIA headquarters in Washington, D.C., about a young teacher in Chinle, Arizona, who had taken a keen interest in learning the Navajo language and culture. Officials contacted me and offered to pay me to spend the summer of 1972 taking post-graduate coursework toward a master's degree in bilingual and bicultural education at the University of Northern Arizona in Flagstaff. They wanted my classroom to become a model for the new pilot program in bilingual education.

I accepted their offer. But, while I learned some interesting information about linguistics, spending two months indoors talking about theory was challenging for me. I missed my life with the Navajo people, and I couldn't wait to return to Chinle.

That fall, I began my second year of teaching. What I had learned over the summer at the university about implementing bilingual and bicultural education in the classroom was not much different from what I had already been doing on my own. But now I had the green light to do even more.

With great enthusiasm, I tried to encourage in the children a sense of cultural pride and self-esteem as Navajo people. I lined the walls in the classroom with pictures of Indian heroes.

My lessons in Indian history and awareness were quite basic, beginning with the names of some of the more famous tribes and their leaders, and then focusing specifically on the Navajo tribe. Although the students were curious about the other tribes we talked about, they did not identify with any of them. They told me they were not Indians. They were *Diné*, which means "The People." They referred to their land as *Dinétah*, literally meaning "among the people."

In those days, Navajos speaking in their own language referred to themselves as *Diné*. When speaking in English, they referred to themselves as *Navajo*. The word *Navajo* is what the Spanish colonizers called them. The origin of the term is believed to be from the Tewa Pueblo word *navahu'u*, meaning "farm fields in the valley."

The Spanish recognized that the Navajo and Apache tribes were closely related. Both of their languages have the same Athabascan roots. The Spanish called the *Diné* the *Apaches de Navajo*—"the Apaches who farm in the valley." Eventually this was shortened to *Navajo*, a term that has persisted throughout the centuries.

I filled the bulletin boards with pictures and facts about Navajo land and history. The children, in turn, gave me lessons in Navajo language and culture. The exchange served as an effective way to teach English painlessly.

The children loved to write stories about their lives. They sometimes illustrated their stories with intricate drawings of animals, canyons, and hogans. I found their stories fascinating, especially those about their experiences with werewolves and witchcraft, both prominent elements of the Navajo belief system.

Donna Scott with her reading group

Once a week, we spent the afternoon in the library. The children loved looking through the books and deciding which ones to check out. Each time we went, one of the students, Johnny Charley, randomly picked out a book and asked me to read it to him.

At 13, Johnny Charley was the second-oldest student in our fourth-grade class. He'd had to stay out of school for several years to help his family with their cattle. Johnny Charley had a great desire to learn. I made an exception to the rule of silence in the library and read to him softly in the corner of the room, trying not to disturb the other students. He put his chair right next to mine. He stared at me as I read. When I looked over at him, he quickly looked away.

Johnny Charley learned so quickly that he soon became one of the top students in my class. He had high aspirations and wanted to be a medicine man someday, like his grandfather.

Near the end of my first year of teaching, the students had made tremendous progress in speaking and writing in English. While the girls excelled in language arts, many of the boys excelled in math and learned the subject with ease. Since every math lesson also served as a language lesson, the boys became fluent in English as well.

Some of the girls had become so proficient in language arts that I entered them in a regional speech contest at Many Farms, Arizona. Four of them won awards for poetry, excellence in original speech, and reading. The whole class felt proud of the girls and proud of themselves.

Most of my time on the reservation was happy and full of wonder. I spent weekends exploring the canyon, participating in ceremonies, or taking the students on trips.

Sometimes I drove by myself to remote wilderness areas in neighboring Utah and Colorado to explore the backcountry. On a few occasions I drove to Taos, New Mexico, to ski in the Sangre de Cristo Mountains.

During my first year of teaching, I had become close friends with Donna Scott. She introduced me to her family, including her brother, R. C. Gorman, a famous artist living in Taos who had achieved national recognition for his paintings of traditional Native women.

R.C. Gorman invited me to stay at his beautiful home during the three weekends that I spent skiing in Taos. He was a flamboyant character who liked to indulge in life's pleasures. I ate lavish meals at his home. In the evenings his driver took us to extravagant parties, where I met celebrities who were his friends.

I felt out of place in my dusty jeans and sneakers and my unsophisticated ponytail. I didn't own any fancy clothes. In fact I hardly had any material possessions.

The glamorous life of Donna's brother stood in stark contrast to the austerity of Navajo life to which I had grown accustomed. In R.C. Gorman's company, I felt like a pauper, yet on the reservation I felt truly wealthy, even though I only made $6,000 per year as a schoolteacher.

After each trip, I welcomed my return to Chinle, where life was simple and without pretense.

In the mornings before going to the classroom, I jogged along the dirt roads and among the red rock formations while I watched the sun rise over the desert. The running served as a form of prayer, a time of giving thanks for being alive in this beautiful land with my students, each of whom I loved as though they were part of my own family.

A Navajo friend who caught glimpses of me running said jokingly, "*Bilagaana, t'oo diigiiz,*" which translates as "white people are really crazy." He said that white people don't have enough physical work to do, so they have to create work for themselves.

On two or three occasions I went to the Saturday evening dances in the public high school auditorium out of curiosity. I wanted to learn more about the Navajos who lived in town. I knew that their lives were vastly different from the lives of the boarding school kids and their families.

People of all ages, ranging from teens to middle age, danced country-western swing to the music of Willie Nelson and Waylon Jennings blasting through the loudspeakers. High school girls often danced with each other, too shy to dance with the boys. A few times a bold young man in cowboy boots and a cowboy hat stepped forward and asked me to dance. We barely exchanged any words and only made fleeting eye contact while dancing. At the end of each dance, we returned to our respective sides of the auditorium, girls on one side, boys on the other.

The more I immersed myself in Navajo life, the better I understood the culture and the meaning of certain behaviors, some of which had initially caused misunderstandings.

Navajo friends and acquaintances often came to my house to borrow money. It gradually dawned on me that they would never pay back what I thought was a loan. I learned that in the Navajo way, people share their possessions. The people whom I knew were not possessive. If they had something others wanted, they readily shared it. Since I was so much a part of Navajo life, they expected the same from me.

Traditional Navajos seemed to have no desire to get ahead of the pack through material wealth or career success. Individuality was subordinate to the community good. My students told me that if a person became too wealthy or successful, he or she would be a target for witchcraft. Ambition to get ahead was not considered an admirable trait among traditional Navajos.

CHAPTER 7
The Puberty Ceremony

In the early spring of my first year at the boarding school, one of the Navajo teacher's aides in the sixth grade classroom, Phyllis Benally, invited me to go with her to visit her large, extended family up on Black Mountain.

The family lived in a compound made up of a cluster of hogans and cinderblock houses, corrals, and shade houses. A dozen children of all ages ran around the compound. Traditional Navajos consider cousins the same as brothers and sisters, making it difficult for my non-Navajo mind to sort out who belonged with whom. The family's proud, handsome 75-year-old grandfather still herded the sheep.

I spent many happy weekends up on the mountain. I helped with the cooking, rode horses, and played with the children, all the while observing Navajo life.

I especially enjoyed riding off with the boys to hunt for the horses and cattle. Normally, boys and girls engaged in separate activities. I was an oddity because I readily joined the boys in their adventures. They loved to tease me. They challenged me to ride certain horses known to be mean-spirited to see if I would get bucked off. I eagerly accepted their challenges, wanting to show them that girls could be just as good at riding bareback as the boys.

One time I accepted the boys' challenge to get on a bull. The bull whirled around, twisted, and kicked his hind legs. After a few seconds, the bull threw me off his back. I landed on a cactus bush. Excruciating pain coursed through my backside while the boys doubled over laughing.

Old abandoned hogan

One of the girls on Black Mountain, Judy, got her period for the first time and was due to have a four-day puberty ceremony, called a *Kinaaldá,* to which I had been invited.

For a few days before the ceremony, according to custom, Judy ran twice a day—once at about five in the morning when it was still dark, and once at noon. I ran with her.

The ceremony was highly ritualized, with strict rules to follow. Judy was not supposed to laugh or eat anything sweet during the ceremony. She had to fix her hair in a certain way, with half of it pulled back and tied with a leather strip made from a mountain lion hide. The hair in front hung down, lining her face. This was supposed to prevent her from going bald when she got older.

Judy dressed in her finest traditional outfit. Her mother combed her hair with thin sticks tied together and then adorned her with almost every piece of jewelry the family owned. She had three turquoise bracelets, two silver concho belts, three necklaces, a pair of earrings, and rings on every finger except her index fingers and thumbs. Navajos don't wear rings on the index finger—at least not while they are alive. After they die, they may be buried with rings on that finger.

I wanted to take a picture of Judy in her finery, but the medicine man told me in a firm voice to put away my Instamatic camera during the *Kinaaldá* ceremony.

Judy spent much of each day of the ceremony on her knees grinding kernels of corn, using the traditional *metate*, or stone grinder. She had to turn many sacks of corn into flour. When she was grinding, she was not supposed to drink any water in order to prevent her breasts from becoming too large when she got older.

The most physically active part of the ceremony came on the third day. The men began digging a wide hole in the ground several yards in front of the hogan. The hole turned into a pit about four feet in diameter and about eight inches deep. The men laid dried juniper branches in the pit, along with a pile of twigs, and started a bonfire.

While the men prepared the fire, the women made corn mush by pouring pails of hot water into a big cauldron with Judy's ground-up corn.

Standing nearby, I saw some of the women chewing on kernels of corn and then spitting the corn into a pail. One of the English-speaking women caught the look of surprise on my face and explained that chewing the corn and mixing it with saliva converted the corn into sugar.

After the women finished chewing the corn and spitting, they dumped the contents of the pail into the corn mush, making it extra sweet. The women stirred the corn concoction with slender sticks tied together, according to ancient protocols.

After many hours of preparation, the mixture was ready for cooking. The fire in the pit had burned the wood down to hot coals. The women removed the coals so they could carefully line the pit with cornhusks to keep the corn mush from getting contaminated with dirt. Then they poured the corn mush into the cornhusk-lined pit.

The men stepped in and laid cornhusks on top of the corn mush in a ritualized fashion, aligned with the direction of the sun's trajectory. The medicine man took a pinch of corn pollen out of his leather pouch and said a blessing while sprinkling the sacred pollen to the four directions. After the blessing, the men shoveled dirt over the top layer of cornhusks and placed the hot coals back on top of the dirt. They added more dried juniper branches to the hot coals to keep the fire burning all night while the corn cake slowly baked in the earthen oven.

At about 10 p.m. the singing began, followed by a ceremony performed by the medicine man with drumming and chanting. The smell of burning sage and sacred tobacco filled the hogan. At midnight we had a break for eating, then the mesmerizing chanting continued for the rest of the night. I had a hard time staying awake.

Around four in the morning, the women washed Judy's hair and her jewelry in a tightly woven basket. They used soap made from pounded yucca root fibers mixed with water. With her hair still wet, Judy ran into the desert, yelling all the while, according to tradition. Anyone could run with her as long as Judy remained in the lead. The women told me that if anyone overtook her, that person would die before she did.

When the sun appeared on the horizon, the women removed the ashes from the fire, peeled away the cornhusks, and cut the ceremonial puberty cake, called *alkaan*, into large chunks.

Judy took the first chunk and put it into her Navajo wedding basket. She broke off a piece and gave it to me. It tasted sweet and delicious.

The ceremony had particular significance for me because I had always felt that most white people—other than Jews, who have bat and bar mitzvahs— sorely lacked initiation rituals to mark the important milestones in life, like puberty and menopause. These Navajo ceremonies were beautiful celebrations of the cycle of our lives, and reminders of our connection with the natural world.

Back in the classroom on Monday morning, I couldn't wait to tell my students about the *Kinaaldá* ceremony. A few of the older girls who had already reached puberty smiled with recognition and nodded their heads.

I excitedly told some of the teachers at the boarding school about my weekend on Black Mountain. They listened with bemusement.

One of my fellow white teachers, a woman in her mid-fifties, thought I had become too much like the Navajo people—content with the status quo, with no interest in getting ahead and rising in the ranks. When I signed a contract to teach a second year at the BIA boarding school, she took me aside and said, "I can't understand why you stay here on the reservation. You could have a great future—unlike those of us who are just waiting to retire and move back home. You could go on and get your PhD in education and be a professor at a college somewhere. You don't seem to have any ambition."

No ambition? No one had ever said that to me before.

CHAPTER 8

Terror off the Reservation

Winter 1972

Being a young, single woman required a certain amount of caution on my part. Men, both white and Navajo, sometimes interpreted my friendliness as an invitation for sex. All too frequently, someone would knock on my door in the dead of night.

One of those times, a drunken man came to my front door and pounded furiously, waking me up in a fright. He yelled in Navajo, "I know you are in there. Let me in." I held my breath, hoping I had re-membered to lock the door before I went to bed, terrified that the man might break into the house. After a few minutes, the yelling stopped and silence returned.

Just as I started to relax again, I heard the intruder outside the back door of my tiny apartment. He banged on the window right above the mattress on the floor where I lay. Before I could jump up and call the Navajo police, he yelled, "If you don't let me in, I'm going to smash the window." And that's exactly what he did.

The window came crashing onto the mattress, shattering into hundreds of shards as the glass hit my body. My neighbor, an administrator at the boarding school, rushed over after hearing my screams. By the time she arrived, the drunken man had disappeared.

My neighbor drove me 40 miles in the night to Sage Memorial Hospital in Ganado to have the innumerable glass splinters removed from my scalp, back, and arms where they had caused considerable pain and bleeding. The next morning, the man's family drove him to the same hospital to have his gashes stitched up. We ran into each other in the hallway of the hospital. While the man looked down at the floor, his family apologized to me and said they had already made arrangements to have my window repaired.

The neighbor who drove me to the hospital informed me that I should hang a curtain over the window next to the shower in the bathroom. She said that even though the window was frosted, people outside could still see the silhouette of the person in the shower.

In the evenings, around the time I took my bedtime shower, she had seen pickup trucks parked outside my apartment. I found this piece of information hard to believe. The next night, I peeked out my window and saw two pickup trucks parked directly facing my house with men sitting in the drivers' seats. From then on, I showered in the dark until I could find a piece of cloth to use as a curtain.

Navajo men were usually gentle and respectful. But I learned that under the influence of bootlegged alcohol—purchased off the reservation—many could become aggressive and unpredictable.

During my years living with the Navajo people, I heard several terrifying stories about young Native women who were assaulted by men off the reservation.

I knew of a few women who traveled to towns off the reservation to run errands or make family visits and ended up raped and beaten. One of them was murdered. In most cases, the men were not prosecuted. Often the traumatized women felt so deeply ashamed about what happened to them that they didn't press charges. They didn't want anyone to know.

One of the most terrifying experiences of my life occurred when one of my Navajo friends invited me to join her for the weekend on a shopping trip to a nearby town off the reservation. After checking into our hotel, we wandered around town. We saw a flyer notifying the public of a country-western dance that night with live music at a well-known bar. We both enjoyed dancing and decided to go.

At the bar, we ordered chips and salsa and two bottles of Pabst Blue Ribbon. I nursed my beer through the entire evening because I knew I couldn't think clearly when I drank even small amounts of alcohol. I had a feeling that on this particular evening, I needed to keep my wits about me.

I watched my friend as she drank a second and then a third bottle of beer. She was losing her natural reserve and was talking and dancing with the men at the bar with abandon.

Two white men sat down at our table and started flirting with my friend. They didn't bother flirting with me because I was obviously sober and keeping a watchful eye on the situation.

There was an aggressiveness about the way the men spoke and behaved that made me feel unsafe. After about a half-hour, the men said they wanted to take us to a private party out in the country to "have some fun." My friend, now intoxicated, agreed to go with them. I spoke to her in Navajo, telling her adamantly that these men were bad people and that we must not go with them. In an uncharacteristically hostile tone, she said, "Look, don't tell me what to do. You don't have to come if you don't want to."

Although I had an intense feeling of foreboding and doom, I could not leave my friend alone with those two white men who gave me the impression that they were capable of doing something very bad. I knew I would regret it for the rest of my life if she were harmed and I had not tried to protect her.

We all piled into the front seat of the men's pickup truck. I sat pressed up against the door on the passenger side. My friend sat between the two men. After we drove away from the bar, I noticed that we were heading away from town. The road was bumpy, full of potholes, and dark, without streetlights. There were no other cars on the road. The man beside me tried to allay my concerns by reminding me that the party was outside of town in the country.

About ten miles out of town, the men said they needed to stop and take a leak. They huddled together in the dark and whispered to each other. Their voices were too low for me to understand. I told my friend in Navajo that I was scared the men were going to harm us. I tried to talk her into getting out and running away, but it was too late—the men climbed back into the truck.

One of the men said they wanted to have sex with us. I lied and said that we had boyfriends who would get very mad if we did anything with other men. Right after I said that, the man next to me lit a cigarette and began to burn the hair on my arm and laugh as I pushed his hand away. The man driving stopped the car and said to my friend, "I'm gonna kill you, bitch."

I tried to get out of the truck, but I couldn't open the door on my side. The handle was broken. My friend jumped out on the driver's side, but the driver pounced on her and knocked her onto the ground. I saw him pounding her face with his fists and ripping off her clothes.

The man next to me got out of the truck on the driver's side and dragged me out with him. Within seconds of landing on the ground, he tried to knock me down. I held onto the side of the pickup truck with my left arm while he twisted my right arm behind my back and pulled my hair so that my head almost touched my arm in back. It was excruciatingly painful. I screamed "You've broken my neck!" And then I went limp, feigning paralysis.

The man loosened his grip briefly, just enough time for me to spin around to free my twisted arm and yank myself out of his grasp. In the ensuing struggle, I managed to wriggle out of my bulky, unzipped ski parka, which he had grabbed onto. Once I had freed myself, I ran for my life into the raw winter night, clad only in a short-sleeved shirt, slacks, and flimsy little party shoes that looked like ballet slippers.

Just before I escaped, I saw my friend being violently raped on the cold pavement, a few yards from the truck. The rapist repeatedly slapped her face and cursed her as he thrust his body into her.

I ran faster than I ever had in my life, my heart pounding, gasping for breath, praying I wouldn't stumble and fall in the darkness or twist my ankle. I could hear my pursuer's footsteps close behind. He yelled and cursed me, letting me know all the hideous things he was going to do to me when he caught me.

After a few minutes, the distance between the man and me increased. I felt my chest was going to burst. The cold air burned my lungs. I jumped into a ditch beside the road and crouched beneath the tumbleweed. The man did not see me and kept running past.

A little farther down the road, he stopped, then walked back to the truck. I held my breath as he walked past my hiding place. He yelled to his partner that I had gotten away. His partner shouted back that they had to find me.

Soon afterward, I saw the headlights on the truck. The men drove toward me. I crouched even lower in the ditch. The truck passed by, and I thought for a moment that I was safe—but then the truck returned. This time, the driver pointed the truck sequentially in each of the four directions so that the headlights could scan the surrounding countryside. I was well camouflaged underneath the tumbleweed. They finally drove away.

When they were out of sight, I began to run again, both to keep from freezing to death and also to keep from being found. To my horror, I saw the lights of the truck approaching yet again. There was no place for me to hide. I lay on the frozen ground a few feet from the side of the road. The truck stopped several yards down the road from me.

Eventually they drove away.

I began running again, this time well away from the road. I ran through the dried-up cornfields, often tripping and falling and getting stabbed in the legs by cornstalk stubble. The moon came out from behind the clouds and gave faint illumination to the land. I was filled with horror. I imagined I was a Jew being hunted by the Nazis—a recurrent dream I'd had while living in Germany during my high school years.

I tried to hum songs to myself to give me courage and subdue the terror. I ran and I ran. I ran in the direction of town, not daring to stop.

I ran until the first light of dawn, when I saw a factory in the distance. I walked up to the chain-linked fence surrounding the factory and breathlessly yelled for help. A guard looked at me suspiciously but then let me in when I yelled that my friend had been raped and beaten.

I was half-frozen and bedraggled, with a ripped shirt and pants and blood on my bare forearms from falling so many times. The guard threw a blanket around my shivering body, gave me hot coffee, and called the police, who appeared almost immediately.

I was relieved to see my friend sitting in the back seat of the police car. Her face was badly bruised and swollen. She had on a long, dark, un-familiar-looking skirt. She expressed surprise at seeing me, thinking that my neck had indeed been broken and that I was still lying in a ditch beside the road.

I joined her in the back of the police car. As we hugged each other, she whispered in my ear that she didn't want the police to know she had been raped because she felt ashamed. She told them she had merely been beaten. She asked that they not press charges if the men were found, because she was afraid they would stalk her and kill her in revenge. She had already divulged information in the bar about her address and place of employment, so tracking her down would be a simple matter.

We drove with the policemen to the scene of the crime on the country road outside of town. We found the spot with no trouble. My blue ski parka lay in the middle of the dirt road. The distance to the scene of the crime from the factory was almost 20 miles, the length of which I had run the night before.

After we finished filling out the paperwork at the police headquarters, the police took us to pick up my friend's car, still parked at the bar where our fateful encounter had begun.

My friend insisted on driving us home herself, in spite of her state of agitation and her bruised and swollen face. As her hands gripped the steering wheel, she recounted to me what had happened to her the night before.

She said that after the men gave up on finding me and drove off with her, they told her they were going to kill her and dump her body off beside the road. She quickly invented a story that her father was a Navajo policeman with connections to the FBI. She convinced the men that if they killed her, her father would catch them at any cost. She swore that she wouldn't tell the police if they let her go.

Through tears, my friend went on to say that the men dropped her off at the edge of town, then drove off. From the waist down, she had on only her torn underpants and her party shoes. She walked up to the first house she saw and rang the doorbell. The intense cold she experienced outweighed her feelings of embarrassment.

A startled woman answered the doorbell. She took my friend inside, gave her of hot coffee and a long wool skirt to cover her bare legs, and then called the police. They picked her up at the house and took her to their headquarters for questioning.

While they were at the headquarters, the police received a call from the factory night watchman regarding a woman in distress.

After telling her story to me, my friend pulled over to the side of the highway, turned off the engine, and sobbed with her face in her hands. I reached over and stroked her shoulder. She pushed my hand away and said, "Don't touch me. I feel dirty."

I asked her why she felt shame about being sexually assaulted, since it wasn't her fault. She let out a bitter little laugh and said that maybe it was her fault. Her Catholic boarding school for girls had taught her all about shame and guilt. She wiped her eyes with the back of her hand and then started up the engine and pulled back onto the highway. We drove the rest of the way home in silence.

My friend never again mentioned the beating and rape. I wanted so badly to help her through her pain, but she wouldn't allow any mention of what we had been through that Saturday night. "I just want to forget that it ever happened," she said.

My heart ached for my friend. Over the next few months, her infectious laugh and beautiful smile disappeared, replaced by a vacant look on her face. The warmth and spontaneity of our friendship shifted into a more restrained relationship.

I would have given anything to help my traumatized friend. I offered to cover the cost of a traditional Navajo ceremony, called the Blessing

Way, to help her retrieve her soul and heal her invisible wounds and restore her back to harmony in the world. She rejected the idea, not wanting anyone to know what happened.

I have honored her request for anonymity by changing every identifying piece of information in this recounting of that terrifying night. Sadly, this incident is not unique to my friend. The number of rapes, murders, and unexplained disappearances of Native women across the country is alarmingly high.

While grieving over the heartbreaking damage done to my friend's spirit, I dealt with my own demons. For the following few weeks, I woke up several times each night with shortness of breath, jaw clenched, shivering and shaking from reliving the terror and the freezing cold.

As soon as I returned home from our ill-fated trip, I sat down on the floor in front of my upright loom and began weaving to calm my agitated mind, as the tears rolled down my cheeks. The rhythmic and repetitive hand movements and sounds of the hardwood comb tapping the weft down tightly into the warp had a hypnotic effect on my mind, creating a sense of peace.

I loved to weave. I had already woven five rugs in the style of Navajo saddle blankets and had almost completed my sixth.

One of the Navajo families in town whom I frequently visited had urged me to learn how to weave, especially if I wanted to "find a good Navajo man to marry." The father, Hastiin, and his brother had built me an upright, freestanding Navajo loom in my little apartment. It stood at the foot of my mattress on the floor.

The mother, Asdza, and her daughters taught me how to card wool from their relatives' Churro sheep, which had been sheared in the spring. Weavers use carding tools to brush the wool to remove any remaining dirt and to align the fibers in preparation for spinning.

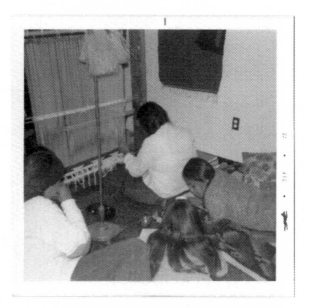

My friends taught me how to weave.

The most difficult part of weaving was spinning the wool into yarn with the drop-down spindle, which I twirled with my right hand against my thigh. When I had spun enough wool, Asdza wound the yarn up and down in large loops on the loom to make the warp.

Since I hadn't yet learned about the plants that I would need for dyeing the yarn, Asdza supplied me with dyed yarn from her own stash. She also gave me handmade wooden tools for weaving, including a thick comb for packing down the yarns that crossed in and out of the warp.

During my two years as a teacher at the boarding school, I wove eight Navajo rugs. I usually wove in the evenings as a way to end my day and clear my mind before preparing for bed.

While exploring the vast and beautiful Navajo Nation, I bought a few stunning Navajo rugs at various trading posts, including the Hubbell Trading Post, famous for its 100-year-old history and its treasure trove of old Navajo jewelry and rugs. Another source of Navajo rugs came from gifts. During some of my weekend visits to my students' hogans, a mother or grandmother would shyly present me with a handsome rug with intricate designs she had woven. I treasured those Navajo rugs.

One of the eight Navajo rugs that I wove with guidance from friends

Weaving wasn't the only diversion I used to clear my mind. Traditional Navajo dancing, with its repetitive two-steps in the Round Dances and the hypnotic drum beat in the background, provided a sure way to calm my mind of troubling thoughts.

On several weekends, I danced during the night in the *Nidaa'*, the Enemy Way Ceremony, a healing ceremony for the Navajo warriors returning from their service in Vietnam. These ceremonial dances were referred to as "Squaw Dances"—a term incorrectly coined by white people but later adopted by Navajos. They served as a place where young single people could meet and get to know each other.

Although I never entered into a romantic relationship with any of the men at the ceremonial dances I attended, I did meet a handsome older Navajo man who caught my attention. He walked unexpectedly into my life at the beginning of my second year of teaching school.

CHAPTER 9

My Friend Marshall

I first met Marshall Tome when he came to the Chinle Boarding School to interview some of the staff. He was writing a story for the newspaper he had founded, *The Navajo Times*, one of the few independent Native newspapers in the country.

Marshall spoke English flawlessly, without a trace of the Navajo accent that I had grown accustomed to hearing among my students and friends—an accent that had unintentionally crept into my own speech.

After the interview, Marshall said he wanted to get together and talk some more. He asked for my telephone number. He was not shy. Marshall pursued me with a surprising persistence. At 50, he was more than twice my age.

After several engaging telephone conversations, I agreed to meet him for lunch.

Marshall lived in Window Rock, Arizona, capital of the Navajo Nation. He was an official in the tribal government in addition to his work as a journalist.

Marshall drove 70 miles from Window Rock to Chinle to have lunch with me. We ate red chili stew and fry bread at Fleming Begay's, the local teachers' hangout and the only restaurant in town. At my urging, Marshall told me about his life. He spoke in a calm and gentle voice.

Having served in World War II, Marshall took advantage of the G.I. Bill, which paid for his college education. He graduated from the University of Missouri with a degree in journalism. Around this time, Marshall married a white woman. They raised two children together, Deswood and Desbah.

While Marshall was working as assistant city editor of the *San Francisco Chronicle* in the 1950s, Navajo officials asked him to return to the Navajo Nation and help his people turn their little newsletter into a real newspaper—*The Navajo Times*. Marshall agreed and returned in 1959 to a job at half his former pay and temporarily without a place to live.

A few years after Marshall returned to his people, his wife left him and their two young children and returned to her home in the Midwest. Marshall told me this information without even a trace of rancor in his voice toward his wife for bailing out.

Our first encounter led to many more lunches. Eventually I agreed to spend the weekend with Marshall in Window Rock, willingly letting myself be pulled into his orbit, seduced by his kindness and intelligence—and his gentle brown eyes.

I made certain Marshall understood that I was not cut out to be his wife or the mother of his children. I was too young and wanted to explore the world. I reminded him that I had already experienced marriage and divorce while in college.

Marshall asked me about my three-year marriage to Jeff Elliott and wanted to know if we still had feelings for each other. I gave him a glimpse of that time in my life to assure him that I didn't have any unfinished business I needed to tend to.

Jeff and I had met during my freshman year at Antioch, a radically progressive college in Yellow Springs, Ohio. I had come from a straight-laced American high school in Germany, unprepared for coping with total freedom. We both were lost souls looking for an anchor. We found refuge in our marriage while chaos and upheaval swirled around us during the mid-sixties. When we each eventually found our footing, our paths diverged in different directions.

In spite of our love for each other, Jeff and I both realized that we had outgrown the confines of marriage. At the time of graduation we separated, reassuring ourselves that we would get back together again after we "found ourselves." After a year apart, we divorced. We remained friendly from a distance, only occasionally seeing each other in person.

Marshall listened attentively. He seemed reassured that there were no loose ends and no surprises in store for him.

One day Marshall asked me if I would like to meet his parents. In white culture, an invitation to meet the parents usually means that the relationship has become more serious. Since Marshall navigated both cultures with ease, I couldn't tell if his question had any extra meaning attached to it. But my curiosity about his parents overruled any concerns about getting too serious.

The next weekend we drove to a vast expanse of stunningly beautiful land called *Red Rock*—eventually renamed *Red Valley*—located just inside the Arizona border. We drove through the nearest town, Shiprock, New Mexico. Although his parents' house was only 30 miles from Shiprock, that leg of the journey took over an hour by pickup truck because of the deeply rutted dirt road that stretched for miles after leaving the paved highway.

Marshall's father, Lee Tome, was tall and slim, with perfect posture, and still agile at age 87. He had served as a councilman for the tribe in his younger years.

Marshall's mother, Virginia Tome, was not exactly sure of her age. Marshall guessed she was in her early eighties. Her eyes looked like she was constantly squinting from the sun, even when she was inside the dimly lit cabin. Her spine curved in her upper back, giving away her age. Both of Marshall's parents still rode horses and engaged in all the heavy labor demanded of them by their rustic lifestyle. Marshall told me they had raised 12 children.

One of their sons, Morris, lived with them in their log cabin. Morris had no idea how old he was, but I guessed that he was around 60. Marshall said that Morris had left home when he was 20 to work in California and Idaho picking potatoes, irrigating farmland, and doing other kinds of migrant work. Over time he got very run down, and then became sick with tuberculosis and had to convalesce in a sanitarium in Albuquerque. He returned home four years later to help his parents with their livestock. Marshall said that Morris had never been to school and only knew a few words of English. He rarely spoke at all.

Virginia and Lee Tome lived in a magnificent part of the Navajo Nation, near the foot of Shiprock, a soaring red rock formation created by volcanic activity. Rows of black boulders that had spewed out in ancient times stretched out for miles, surrounded by an ocean of treeless desert. The Lukachukai and Carrizo Mountains loomed in the near distance, while the snow-covered La Plata Mountains majestically presided far to the northeast in southern Colorado.

Brilliant blue sky stretched to infinity. The desert air was intoxicating with the pungent, purifying scent of sagebrush. Smoke from burning piñon pine and cedar in the wood stove smelled like incense.

Only a handful of families lived with their livestock in this pristine and sparsely inhabited land. Because of the remoteness of the area and the difficulty of access, life in the Red Rock area had probably not changed much from the late 1800's—rugged, simple, and in close harmony with the land.

During my first visit, I felt such a powerful attraction to this land that I vowed to myself I would find a way to live there someday.

Marshall was pleased that I took such a liking to his ancestral home. At my request, we returned to Red Rock three or four more times to visit his family. I enjoyed exploring the area. We hiked among the rock formations, drove to the Red Rock Trading Post, and talked with the trader about his life serving the Navajo people in the area. I rode horseback with Marshall's young children, Desbah and Deswood, who joined us on a couple of the visits.

My friend Marshall

On one of the visits, I counted 597 sheep and goats in the corral. Lee Tome's livestock also included a herd of cows and a few horses. By traditional Navajo standards, Lee Tome was a wealthy man. Marshall said that at one time his father owned well over one thousand sheep and goats, but had to sell half of his herd because of the government's concerns about overgrazing.

I had never encountered this kind of wealth among the families I had visited with my students. Some of the families who lived in remote areas were desperately poor and without livestock. They relied on help from relatives and the local churches just to survive.

After my third visit, I attempted to have a conversation with Virginia and Lee Tome in Navajo. But I ran out of things to say after about ten minutes of asking basic questions like, "What are the names of your dogs? How many children do you have? How many sheep? How many goats? Do you have cows? How far away is the trading post? Where do you get your water from?" I said their land was beautiful, and I thanked them for the food they gave me to eat. I added that I liked their horses. They laughed while I struggled to continue the conversation. They spoke only a few words of heavily accented English, like "ships" for sheep, "coos" for cows, and "wabie" for water. After I ran out of things to say in Navajo, we didn't speak at all and just sat together in a timeless state of silence.

Seeing my eagerness to learn more about Navajo language and culture, Marshall suggested that I spend time living with his parents to truly immerse myself in traditional life and become more conversant in Navajo. I thought about his suggestion, imagining myself herding sheep. It sounded like a great idea. The school year was almost over, so I could start at the beginning of June.

Marshall told his family about my desire to herd sheep and get a close-up view of traditional Navajo life. His parents sat in silence for a few long moments and then both of them burst out laughing at the same time. When they realized that Marshall spoke in earnest, they began discussing among themselves the unusual request. Marshall told me they needed time to think about it.

Morris was the family's sheepherder. A few weeks after Marshall proposed to his parents that his white schoolteacher friend could herd their sheep, Morris decided to retire from sheepherding and agreed to give me his job. His parents offered to pay me $100 a month, along with some priceless old Navajo silver and turquoise jewelry, in exchange for herding their 597 sheep and goats.

By the time the school year ended, I had made up my mind not to return that summer to the University of Northern Arizona to complete my master's degree in bilingual and bicultural education, as previously planned. Instead, I decided to become a sheepherder in Red Rock, Arizona.

My colleagues at the boarding school thought I must have lost my mind. They grilled me with questions. "Why in the world do you want to spend the summer herding sheep in the middle of nowhere? Why don't you want to complete your master's degree—especially since the government offered to cover all your expenses?"

In contrast to the reaction of my colleagues, my Navajo friends, along with the students in my class, found the whole idea humorous and intriguing. I thought it would be a brilliant way to spend the summer while becoming more conversant in Navajo and experiencing traditional Navajo life from the inside—not just from inside a classroom at the University of Northern Arizona.

The BIA agreed that I could leave my apartment unoccupied for the summer. When school ended the last week of May, I stuffed my backpack with a few belongings and drove off to begin my new life in a place outside of time.

CHAPTER 10

Herding Sheep

Summer 1973

Life was rugged in Red Rock. We got up at five in the morning with the first light. Virginia Tome told me that if the sun caught a person in bed, that was a sign of laziness. She was strict and critical, but a good teacher of the Navajo Way.

When no one was around, I spoke into my little portable tape recorder. I wanted to give my family a detailed account of my day-to-day life as a sheepherder on the reservation. Through the stories I had told my parents and siblings over the phone while living in Chinle they had grown fond of the Navajo people and wanted to know more about life on the reservation.

July 4, 1973

"Today is Independence Day. Right now I'm by myself in the log cabin. Lee Tome and Morris have gone to Shiprock to get their pickup fixed. Virginia Tome rode off on her horse toward the mountains to check on the cows. I want to take advantage of this opportunity to speak in

English into the tape recorder and tell you about my life in Red Rock. If I sound like I have an odd accent, it's because I'm so used to speaking in Navajo that I catch myself using the same intonation when I speak English.

"I've been living out here herding sheep for a month now. I'm learning a lot of Navajo, but my vocabulary is still limited. Somehow I manage to find a way to express myself even when I can't find the right words.

"Yesterday I wanted to ask Lee Tome about his rifle. Not knowing the Navajo word for *rifle*, I referred to it as 'the long stick that makes a big noise.' Lee and Virginia Tome thought that was funny.

"I haven't spoken very much since I became a sheepherder. Most of the day I have only the sheep and goats and my horse to talk to—and the sheepherding dogs. I talk to all of them in Navajo because it's a good way to practice. The animals don't care if I sound like a two-year-old.

"Virginia Tome said that I talk a lot in my sleep. Some of the words I say are in Navajo. Last night I woke her up when I yelled '*hádi dibé*,' meaning 'where are the sheep?'

"I often dream that I've lost some of the sheep while they're out grazing, and I can't find them. Virginia and Lee Tome would be very upset to lose even one of their sheep.

"Virginia Tome asked me to call her *Shimasani*, meaning 'Grandmother.'

"Grandmother is very strict and tells everyone what to do. Traditional Navajos live in a matriarchal culture. It might look like the men are in charge, but it's really the women who run the show. Marshall told me that in the old days—before the influence of white culture—when a married woman wanted a divorce, she simply put her husband's saddle outside the door of the hogan. That meant her husband could not come back.

"Grandmother is amazingly strong. She rides horseback and does heavy labor even though some people her age would be in an old folks' home.

Virginia Tome continued to ride well into her eighties.

"Lee Tome rides a lot too. He rides like a cowboy and uses a lasso, even at 87 years of age. He has a good reputation around here. The man at the trading post said that as a councilman at the Red Rock Chapter House, Lee Tome had accomplished a lot toward helping his people have a better life.

"Lee Tome used to own most of the Red Rock area, but gradually people moved in and asked him to give them some of his land. So he gave it away, and piece by piece, his land shrunk to what it is now. But by white standards, what he still owns is huge and stretches for miles.

"It is a busy life here. There's no time for play. Even though Window Rock is celebrating the Fourth of July with a rodeo, powwow, and parade—according to the Navajo radio station—Virginia and Lee Tome wouldn't think of going. I volunteered to stay here and watch things for them, but they just can't let themselves take a vacation. They worry too much about all the things they have to do, and they worry if their sheep are all right."

July 13, 1973

"At this moment, I'm sitting on a cot inside the cabin, with the tape recorder in my hand and my bare feet on the dirt floor. Three other cots line the walls, looking like they could have been hospital beds in a makeshift clinic for soldiers in Vietnam.

"With the war finally coming to an end, Vietnam has been on my mind. I haven't watched TV in over two years, but I have seen the Navajo warriors coming home to their families at last—some of them wounded physically and some emotionally and still others coming home in coffins. My heart breaks thinking about it.

"A large gas stove stands in the middle of the east wall of this cabin. On one side of the stove is a folding table where all the cooking supplies are stacked. On the other side is a sink with no water faucet, just a drain that empties outside into a container for catching the dirty water. In the corner is a gas-run refrigerator that the Tomes recently purchased. We eat our meals at a wooden table in the middle of the room. Off to the side, the old cast-iron wood stove warms up the cabin in the chilly early morning before the sun comes up.

"Outside, a shade house attached to the front of the cabin serves as a porch. Branches cover the top of the pine pole structure. Sitting under the shade house offers relief when the sun is beating down hard during the day.

The cabin where we lived had a shaded porch where Grandmother rested when it was too hot to be inside.

"When the nights are very hot, I sleep outside in the shade house. It feels good to sleep on the ground on top of a couple of sheepskins and breathe the cool fresh air. Everyone else is too scared to sleep outside. They're afraid a werewolf might come in the night and do something bad. They marvel that I'm not afraid to sleep out there by myself.

"I usually get up with the rest of the family by five. If Grandmother hasn't already made a fire in the stove, then I make it and put the water on the stove to boil. After that, I run for two or three miles along the dirt road. Running wakes me up, makes me feel good, and keeps me strong. And I get to watch the sun rise on the horizon and light up the land.

"When I come back, I help make breakfast. We usually eat the same thing every day—potatoes fried in a lot of lard, with oatmeal and Navajo coffee boiled in a pot. For a special treat, we sometimes have juice. If there is a guest staying here, we might have fried chicken with fry bread for breakfast, or burned toast. We eat Navajo fry bread with most meals.

"While I wash the dishes and do my other chores, I listen to the Navajo radio station broadcast from Farmington. Lee Tome turns the volume way up. He has trouble with his hearing.

"I have learned a lot of Navajo language by listening to that radio station. They announce the news from the reservation, where the next 'Squaw Dance' is going to be held, where you can find the best bargains in town, and what's going on in the capital of Window Rock. They play Navajo music and sometimes music from other tribes.

"Before we eat breakfast, we wash ourselves. We use water very sparingly. Grandmother allows each of us only one little bowl of water each day for all our hygiene needs—including brushing our teeth, washing our bodies, and rinsing our face. Fortunately, the outhouse is well stocked with sheets of newspaper and a little toilet paper.

"We haul the water in big metal barrels from the tank next to the windmill down the road. The windmill pumps the water out of the ground when the wind blows. Every day I bring the sheep to the windmill, where I can get really clean with the water from the holding tank. If Grandmother saw me 'wasting water,' I bet she'd give me a good scolding.

"Every day, after we eat, I go out and saddle up Jimmy, the sheepherding horse, and then I come back and do the dishes. At first it was hard for me to get used to washing the dishes in a small bowl. No one rinses the soapy dishes because it requires too much water. They simply dry them with a paper towel.

"By the time I finish washing the dishes, the water in the bowl is black. At first I felt like I couldn't eat off those dishes. Now I am used to it. I guess you can get used to just about anything. Besides, no one seems to get sick around here, so I'm guessing that germs are not something I need to worry about.

"After the dishes are done and the cabin is cleaned up, I let the sheep and goats out of the corral. The other day I counted the herd to make sure we still had all of the 597 sheep and goats. I would feel really bad if any of them got lost or eaten by a coyote. And I'd get into a lot of trouble with Grandmother if that happened."

I spent hours on Jimmy's back thinking about life.

July 20, 1973

"A couple weeks ago, we castrated the young male goats and lambs. We put special rubber bands around the base of the balls to cut off the blood supply. After several days, the balls fall off. The same procedure is done on the tails. I don't know the reason for removing the tails except that the trader says this is what must be done if they want to sell the meat at the trading post. The hungry dogs follow behind the sheep, waiting for the balls and tails to fall off so they can eat them.

"I usually herd the sheep for several miles, wherever there are enough plants and grass to eat. Then I take them to the windmill, where the water is pumped into a trough. The herd drinks between one and four times during the day, depending on how hot it is. When they get near the water, they take off running. They are so thirsty it's hard to get them to leave the trough.

Jimmy and the sheep drink at the trough next to the windmill.

"Around midday, I start bringing the sheep home. They huddle under the shade house built for the animals, trying to find relief from the blazing sun. Then I unbridle Jimmy, feed him, and go make lunch. After I've finished eating and washed the dishes, I do whatever needs to be done around the cabin. I might drive Grandmother to the trading post if we need a bag of flour or other supplies.

The sheep huddle under the shade house, trying to cool off.

"Around mid-afternoon, I take the sheep back out again. It's hard to get them away from the shade house. They hate the heat. But once they reach the green plants, they start walking more willingly.

"Lee Tome is having a dispute with one of his relatives. He gave a piece of land to his wife's sister and her family. He told them they could graze their sheep there as long as they did not build on the land. The relatives set up their home there anyway, right near where Lee Tome's sheep used to graze. Now the two families are enemies.

"One of these relatives, Raymond, has been practicing witchcraft. An English-speaking Navajo man told me this information at the Red Rock Trading Post when I went there to buy staples for cooking. The trader said that Raymond has been putting something in the sheep's water that makes them sick.

"Lee and Virginia Tome are terrified of Raymond. They call him 'Weemie.' It's their Navajo way of pronouncing his name. Whenever anything goes wrong, they say that Weemie did it, and then they curse him. '*Weemie, t'oo baa ii. Doo yaa' a shoo da.*' Werewolves and witchcraft are part of life out here."

July 25, 1973

"A few miles down the road west of here, there is a large reservoir stocked with trout. I like to go fishing during my spare time—although there isn't much spare time to be had. Thanks to Marshall's help with negotiations during one of his visits, Virginia and Lee Tome agreed to give me one day off a week. Morris fills in for me on those days.

I'm getting ready to head out with the sheep and goats.

"I went fishing with a young Navajo man who took a shine to me, Robert Henderson. His older brother was a good friend of mine in Chinle. Robert and I brought back two trout—but no one touched them. I got to eat both of them myself for breakfast. Grandmother acted scared when I showed her the fish. She had never seen or tasted fish before and did not want to try it. She seemed upset that I brought Robert to their cabin. She clearly didn't like him. I don't think she liked the idea that I had been with a boy—a boy who was not their son."

July 27, 1973

"The land around here is magnificent. I sit on Jimmy's back for hours while I'm herding the sheep and just marvel at the beauty of the mountains, the red rock formations, and the vast blue sky. On the days I ride bareback, I often lie on Jimmy's back and look up at the shapes of the clouds and watch them drift by overhead.

"While I'm herding the sheep around, I see quite a bit of animal activity—more than one would imagine from looking out onto this seemingly barren land. There are lots of lizards, horned toads, prairie dogs, jackrabbits, coyotes, and rattlesnakes.

"I almost stepped on a rattlesnake on two different occasions while I was walking in rocky areas. Fortunately I heard their warning rattles and got out of the way. It is a startling sight to come upon a coiled rattlesnake ready to strike.

"I have encountered quite a few dead things, like carcasses of sheep, a calf, a cow, and a raven. Grandmother is afraid of the ravens. Whenever she sees one, she says 't'oo baa adzid,' meaning, 'it's really scary.' If a raven hangs around your house, it means someone will die soon, according to Navajo belief.

"The dogs caught and killed a jackrabbit. I brought it home and chopped it up with the axe and parceled it out to the animals around the house—the dogs, cats, and ducks. The animals are always hungry and will eat almost anything.

"Rabbit meat is the dogs' main diet. The scraps at home merely supplement their diet. They catch about one rabbit per day. It's a gruesome sight to see all the dogs gathered around the rabbit, ripping it apart while it's still alive. It makes a pathetic cry that sounds like a whimpering baby. The sound makes my stomach tighten up. I never knew until now that rabbits could vocalize.

"The dogs are always hungry. One of the dogs just had puppies. Morris built the puppies a little house next to the sheep corral so the other dogs won't eat them. When the cat had kittens, the dogs ate them.

"Grandmother doesn't want me to show affection to the dogs because then they just hang around the house. Navajos living on the land don't treat dogs the way white people do. Navajo dogs are not pets. They are not allowed in the house. They are expected to work, herding the sheep and keeping the coyotes away from the sheep corral at night. If they don't fulfill their roles, no one wants them. When they come around sniffing, they get kicked. I saw Morris step on the tail of one of the dogs when he wanted the dog to get out of the shade house.

"There is a real hierarchy among the dogs. *Neez*, meaning 'Tall One,' is the biggest, so he's the boss. Any time one of the dogs does something he doesn't like, he growls, and then the others get so terrified they roll over and show their submission. He gets first choice on everything, especially food.

"Neez has a lot of matted fur. Occasionally I brush his hair with the same currycomb that Lee Tome uses on the horses. A lot of hair comes off with each brushing. He looks like he's part collie, with his long coat. One time, Grandmother saw me trying to brush through the matted fur. She got the big scissors that she uses to shear sheep and started cutting Neez's furry coat. She got so carried away that she ended up cutting off all the fur on his tail, leaving just the skin and a few tufts of hair. Now he looks embarrassed and isn't as bossy with the other dogs.

"Besides Neez, there are two other big sheepherding dogs—Blackie and *Jaayaa Loli*, meaning 'Pointed Ears.' When Grandmother is not looking, I pet them. I try not to do it too often so they won't get too attached to me.

Jaayaa Loli was brought up among the sheep. He spends most of his time with them. Virginia and Lee Tome like him the best. He doesn't come around the house; he doesn't beg; he doesn't jump up on people. He's a real sheep dog. He just comes when he is called to get some scraps of food. Sometimes he gets overexcited about his job of herding sheep and goes overboard, rounding them up constantly. The sheep lose weight from running so much. Just recently, Morris tied a big chain around Jaayaa Loli's neck that the dog drags between his feet, keeping him from running. When he does try to run, the chain flies around and sometimes hits him in the head.

"Grandmother scolds me when I pet the dogs. She says I will ruin her dogs and turn them into *bilagáana* dogs that don't know how to work. One day I made the mistake of telling Lee and Virginia Tome about a sheep that got lost after one of the dogs chased it. Lee Tome asked me which dog chased the sheep. After I told him, to my horror, he tied the dog to a tree and shot it in the head for not doing its job right. I felt awful. I can't get that image out of my mind. I shouldn't have said anything. Life out here can be pretty harsh."

July 29, 1973

"I stay out with the sheep until about eight in the evening. After I bring them back to the corral, I unsaddle and unbridle Jimmy, help make dinner, eat, wash up, chop wood, and light the Coleman lantern, and then we all go and sit out in the shade house. We sit in silence, relaxing and watching the night settle into the desert.

"Evening is the time when Lee Tome pulls out his leather pouch, puts a pinch of tobacco on a square of paper, and rolls a cigarette—his one cigarette of the day. He smokes it sitting in the doorway, looking out into the darkness. This is his cherished moment when he can sit back and relax. He holds the cigarette between his thumb and index finger and smokes the tobacco as though it had some kind of sacred significance. He takes a puff with his eyes closed and then lets the smoke out slowly while looking lovingly at the cigarette between his fingers. Watching him savoring his smoke puts me into a trance-like state and makes me long for a hand-rolled cigarette to smoke the way he does.

"Yikes! I can hear the pickup truck coming toward the cabin. I have to stop recording now. I don't want Grandmother to think I've been idle while she and Lee Tome and Morris were out doing chores. And I have to get on my cowboy boots real quick so Grandmother doesn't think I'm a barefoot hippie. I'll tell you more about the sheepherding life later—like how I butchered my first sheep. Stay tuned."

CHAPTER 11

Butchering Sheep

August 1, 1973

"I'm back again. That's the wind you hear in the background on the cassette tape. The wind blows very hard out here. Sometimes it whips the dust around so ferociously that you can't see even a yard in front of you. The blowing dust would be worse now, except that this year we had heavy rains during the spring. New growth of vegetation keeps down the loose dirt. The wind just now blew an empty pail off the box in front of me.

"A few weeks ago, Grandmother told me I had to learn how to butcher a sheep if I wanted to be a good Navajo wife. I wondered if she meant being a good wife to her son, Marshall.

"Last week I butchered my first sheep. Morris grabbed the sheep's legs, making it fall to its side, and then he tied the legs together. Grandmother brought out her little brown leather pouch of corn pollen. She made a mark with the yellow powder on the sheep's forehead, and then said a prayer, thanking Brother Sheep for giving its life so that her people could go on living. I said my own prayer to the sheep, asking for forgiveness for what I was about to do.

"After the prayer with corn pollen, Grandmother directed me to slice the sheep across its neck. I shut off my feelings and focused all my attention on what Grandmother told me to do. We let the blood drain out into a pan. Grandmother saved the blood for making blood sausage. After the bleeding stopped, I held the sheep's head and extended the neck forcefully against my knee to break apart the vertebrae. Then I cut off the head, following Grandmother's instructions.

"Traditional Navajos eat every part of the sheep. Nothing is wasted. After I severed the head, I cut out the tongue—considered a delicacy—and then I placed the head on the hot coals to roast in the fire pit. The sheep's open eyes gazed up at me from the fire pit. I had to look away and swallow hard. The sight haunted me. As you know, I was a self-righteous vegetarian before I came to live on the reservation.

"Grandmother handed me a rope to suspend the sheep from a tree branch by one of its legs so that the carcass wouldn't get dirty. She gestured that I needed to make a shallow slice from stem to stern on the underside of the sheep. After I made the long slice, she demonstrated how to peel off the hide from the flesh, using her fist to separate the membranes.

"Once we had pulled the sheepskin off, I slit open the now-naked sheep's belly and removed the innards. Grandmother squeezed out onto the ground the green, fibrous contents of the intestines, then washed them in a bowl and prepared them to be cooked and served as tripe.

"The meat located over the breastbone is always reserved for the sheepherder, since it is considered the choicest piece of meat. Fortunately, I preferred this piece. I had a hard time with some of the other parts, especially the brains and the lungs.

"Butchering is a big job. If Grandmother had not insisted, I would not have been willing to butcher the sheep. But I'm glad I had this experience, so that I know exactly what eating meat involves. From now on, I'm going to think about the animal I'm eating and say a silent prayer of thanks.

"After the butchering, we hang the sheepskins on a line to dry. Later, we will tan the hides by rubbing the sheep's brains on the hides, making them soft and pliable. The sheepskins serve as sleeping mats on the dirt floor, or as covers when it's cold.

The skins from the freshly butchered sheep hang to dry.

"When a sheep gets sick, Grandmother goes up to the mountains and finds some special plants that she boils in a certain way. She puts the juice of the medicinal plants in their water and also rubs it on their bodies. Virginia and Lee Tome use plants as medicine, following the old Navajo traditions. Sick sheep usually get well with their concoctions.

"There are two blind goat kids that Grandmother kept in the corral today while I took the rest of the herd out to graze. She had made some Navajo herbal medicine that she rubbed into their eyes. I will find out soon if it was effective. I don't know how much you can do for blind goats."

August 3, 1973

"Four miles from here, at the foot of the Lukachukai Mountains, there is a beautiful lake, called 'Big Gap.' It has far more trout in it than the reservoir down the road. Sometimes my friends from Shiprock come by and ask me to go fishing with them at the lake.

"Grandmother is jealous about how I spend my time—especially when it is with boys. She would rather I stay here with her, even though I am getting paid just for herding sheep. I think she is hoping I will marry her son. I told Marshall to inform his mother that I am only a friend.

"Grandmother is rude to these Navajo boys. One of the long-haired boys greeted Grandmother politely and extended his hand toward her. She refused to shake his hand, calling him a 'tsii yogi,' meaning "hippie." I suspect that Grandmother was upset that the boy wore his long hair loose and unkempt. Traditional Navajo men have their long hair tied neatly in a 'Navajo knot.'

"At first her hostility toward the boys created a big misunderstanding between us. I felt like Grandmother was controlling my life. As a bilagáana, I'm not used to having somebody want me to stay home all the time and try to prevent me from going out with friends on my day off.

"Another point of tension occurs whenever I want to go to the trading post or to Shiprock to buy something I need. When I tell Grandmother, she says 't'oo dini,' which means, 'you're just saying that,' suggesting that I'm lying. I think she suspects that I'm going to meet boys.

"Virginia and Lee Tome have hired quite a few sheepherders in the past. Grandmother said they all lied, got drunk, and ran away. Every time I go someplace, she's afraid I'm not going to come back—just like all the other sheepherders. She acts surprised when I do come back. She probably can't get over the fact that a white woman would want to come way out here and live like a Navajo.

"I know I am the subject of a lot of conversations in the Red Rock area. Sometimes when I'm out with the sheep, I can see people in their pickup trucks stopped by the side of the dirt road, just staring at me for long stretches of time. I don't own a watch, but I would guess they stare for at least an hour sometimes. They probably can't believe their eyes. When I'm at the trading post, I watch people trying to get a look at me without being too obvious. Sometimes the women and girls smile and giggle with their hands over their mouths when I walk by."

August 4, 1973

"In spite of Grandmother's protests, I usually try to get away for a little while on my day off for a change of scene. One weekend I went to a wedding with a Hopi friend of mine at her village high on a cliff.

"The Hopi Reservation is surrounded by the Navajo Nation. Some of the areas overlap, which causes a lot of conflict between the two tribes. In some places, the Navajo families are getting pushed off their ancestral lands. This disaster is related to the way the land was partitioned by the U.S. government.

"Another source of conflict and suffering was caused by a mining company on Black Mesa. The strip mining has profoundly affected both tribes—destroying their land, polluting their water, and forcing some of the families to relocate. My friends who have traveled to Washington to protest this injustice told me that the lawyers who negotiated the agreement with the two tribes lied about the terms. It makes me sick looking at the devastation from the strip mining and knowing how white authorities cheated and lied to the tribes to make a fortune for themselves.

"While I waited for the ceremony to begin, I played outside with the children. A little dog ran over to join in the fun, barking and wagging his tail, but within a few minutes he disappeared. I didn't think anything of it.

"Later that day, we had a big feast after the ceremony. The main dish was a thick stew made out of an unusual kind of meat with an unfamiliar smell. I noticed that the people around the table watched me as I ate. Someone asked me if I thought the stew was good, and then everyone laughed. In that moment, a wave of nausea passed over me as I remembered the little dog. My Navajo friends had told me that the Hopi people sometimes eat dog meat. I politely excused myself, walked to the edge of a nearby cliff where no one could see me, and threw up."

August 6, 1973

"Virginia and Lee Tome are off on their horses now, checking on the cattle. Morris has gone to his irrigated fields in Shiprock, where he grows his own hay for the horses, along with a few rows of melons, squash, and potatoes. This is the perfect time to record this message to you.

"Right now I'm sitting at the little table in the shade house. This is where we eat our meals when it's too hot inside the cabin. I'm looking around, observing my surroundings. A little plastic bag containing dried sheep's brains hangs above me from one of the poles. A bundle of sheepskins and goatskins hangs from the branch of a nearby tree. Off to my right are buckets, stacks of chopped wood, bags of cement, two saddles stacked one on top of the other, a bridle, and a pile of lumber. Just beyond the cabin is a horse trailer. Over to my left are four water barrels, a dipper for the water, and a horsewhip. Underneath my chair are several plastic bags filled with wool that Grandmother spun with her drop spindle. Soon we will dye the wool with the plants she has gathered near the mountains.

"Lee Tome planted two young elm trees in front of the cabin for shade. We pour all the dirty wash water around the base of the trees. I see that the little trees have already grown a few inches during the two months I've been here. Two of Lee Tome's ducks are pecking at the dirt, looking for food. They are good at catching flies and eating them.

"In the distance I can see the windmill about a quarter of a mile down the dirt road. The windmill is where we do all our big washings. I go there on my days off to wash my clothes and hair. It feels so good to have clean hair, a clean body, and clean clothes. That clean feeling usually lasts for only a few hours after I wash, but those few hours are blissful.

"The excess water that comes out of the pump runs off into a little lake. Sometimes the dogs sit in there to cool off on the hot days. It can get killing hot here. Every so often we have to clean out the troughs where the animals drink because the sheep stand in them when they are drinking and poop in the water. Also, there is slimy green stuff like seaweed that comes out of their mouth and makes the water filthy.

"I have to tie Lee Tome's stud up securely when I take him to drink at the trough. If another stud came over to drink, there could be a big fight. I can see a herd of horses that are drinking as I speak. They are someone else's horses, not ours. Out here, most of the horses are allowed to roam around freely, so they give the impression that they are wild horses.

"It's time for me to go take the sheep out again."

I saddled up Jimmy and headed out with the sheep to graze.

"I'm back. I'm talking to you right now from the saddle. Jimmy and I are out herding the sheep and marveling at the scenery. Off to the north are the La Plata Mountains in southwestern Colorado. Just recently, all the snow melted off the peaks. The tallest one is called Mount Hesperus. The Navajo people call it *Dibentsaa*, or 'Big Sheep.' It is one of the four sacred mountains that mark the boundary of the Navajo Nation. Navajos call their land *Diné Bikeyah*, meaning 'The People's Land.'

"In the Navajo creation story, the Holy Ones, the *Yé'ii,* gave the Navajo people their homeland with the four sacred mountains representing the four directions. To the east is majestic Mount Blanca in the Sangre de Cristo Range, known to the Navajo as *Sisnaajini*. To the south is Mount Taylor in New Mexico, known as *Tsoodzil*, meaning 'Big Mountain.' And to the west are the San Francisco Peaks in northwestern Arizona, called *Dook'o'ooslííd* in Navajo.

"Virginia Tome is helping me learn more about Navajo history. She smiled when I pointed with my lips in all four directions to the sacred mountains and said their names in Navajo.

"About a quarter-mile west of here, Virginia and Lee Tome have their hogan, where they used to live before they built their log cabin. These days, the family members use their hogan only for traditional ceremonies."

August 8, 1973

"Last Saturday, when Marshall paid us one of his surprise visits, I asked him to take me to a hair salon in Shiprock. I had decided to cut off my hair because it was too much trouble to keep clean—and my scalp had started to itch.

"As I sat in the chair at the hair salon, I looked into the mirror in front of me. I silently gasped when I saw the white face in the mirror. I keep forgetting that I'm not Navajo.

"I said a bittersweet good-bye to the long, dark clumps of hair that lay scattered on the floor of the hair salon. I haven't had hair this short since I was about ten years old. My Navajo friends in Shiprock are disappointed because now I won't be able to wear my hair in a *tsii yeel*—the traditional Navajo knot worn during special ceremonies.

"The older women wear their long hair in a *tsii yeel* every day. Before I took off for Shiprock, Grandmother let me know that she did not approve of me cutting off my hair. She told me to gather up every last hair cut from my head in the hair salon, and then I was supposed to either burn or bury the hair when I returned home so that no one—like Weemie—could use it for witchcraft against me. I buried the bundle of hair yesterday near some sagebrush not far from the windmill."

I had to get used to having short hair.

August 10, 1973

"I wish you could see the beautiful antique Navajo jewelry I have on. Lee Tome pays my wages partly in jewelry and partly in *béeso*, meaning 'dollar' in Navajo. *Béeso* comes from the Spanish word 'peso.'

"Lee Tome gave me a very old turquoise necklace, a pair of turquoise beaded earrings, and a silver concho belt. I feel regal, even though I'm covered in dirt and dust and my hair is matted like the hair on the sheep dogs. I stood in front of Jimmy this morning and showed off my jewelry. I asked him if he liked it. He snorted and nudged me with his head."

August 11, 1973

"A couple days ago Virginia and Lee Tome rounded up the cows and put them in the corral. Some of their relatives who are cowboys came over to help brand the young calves. We also gave penicillin shots to the ones who had pink eye. Lee Tome takes good care of his livestock. The trader told me he gives the best price for Lee Tome's cattle, sheep, and goats because he takes such good care of them.

"Virginia Tome said she would take me out one day to show me the plants I would need for dyeing the wool for my weavings.

"The sheep and goats are resting in the shade house that Morris built for them. One of the goats wandered off and now he is right in front of me. He jumped up with his front feet braced on the little elm tree. He's chewing off the lower leaves. I better go put him back in the shade house. Lee Tome would not be happy if I let the goat eat his young tree. I'll be back."

CHAPTER 12
They Forget I'm White

August 13, 1973

"I have been here two and a half months now. I am alone in the cabin. The only time I talk into the tape recorder is when I'm alone. I would never do it when Grandmother was around. Once I took her picture with my Instamatic camera. Since then, she always puts her hands over her face when she sees me with the camera, or she turns and walks in another direction. Marshall said that his mother thinks the camera will capture her spirit. But Lee Tome doesn't seem to mind at all when I ask if I can take his picture. He's used to being in public and having his picture taken.

"We were up in the Lukachukai Mountains today. All of the relatives got together and had a big picnic before they went off to gather wood and load it onto their trucks. We filled six pickup trucks with the wood we gathered. The wood has to last through the winter.

"Before we left home this morning, we butchered a goat to take with us to feed all the relatives. I helped prepare the goat meat. I washed the intestines after squeezing out the green contents onto the ground. Following Grandmother's instructions, I cut strips of fat from the meat and then wrapped the strips around the intestines before boiling them. We removed an especially thick piece of fat around the stomach and wrapped it around the liver for cooking.

"I rinsed out the inside of the stomach and filled it with ground corn, sliced potatoes, onions, chopped kidney, and the goat's blood. Then Grandmother showed me how to sew the stomach shut with string. We boiled the stuffed stomach in a large pot for a long time. Grandmother said that if the contents of the stomach are not thoroughly cooked, they can make you sick.

"Grandmother taught me how to make a type of bread called *naaneskadi*. The bread looks like tortillas. We prepare the dough like we do with fry bread, but instead of using grease in a frying pan, we cook the bread on a griddle. I made a batch that got smiles of approval from all the women.

"Lee Tome put the big iron grill on the fire outside, beyond the shade house, and grilled the ribs and liver. Grandmother chopped up some of the meat and put it into a huge pot and cooked it into a delicious stew.

"All the relatives worked together to create a real feast for the picnic today. We even had a salad with iceberg lettuce and jars of purple Kool-Aid that came from the trading post. When we got to the mountains, we laid our Pendleton blankets on the grass under big shade trees in the refreshingly cool, pine-scented air. As we ate, the relatives talked about their day-to-day lives, including the price they were getting for their rugs and the disease going around that was killing the prairie dogs—a valued source of food. And of course, they talked about witchcraft.

"I had to leave everyone and drive home early to take the sheep out to graze. Lee and Virginia Tome are afraid to leave the livestock alone because they think someone might come by and steal some sheep or one of the horses in the corral. Just now, I carefully stacked the wood I gathered in the mountains into a big pile beyond the shade house.

"I have to end here. It's starting to get dark, and Virginia and Lee Tome will be coming back from the mountains any minute. I'll talk more tomorrow when I'm out with Jimmy."

August 14, 1973

"Jimmy is munching on some plants. We're surrounded by a white sea of sheep and goats. The sky is an electrifying blue.

"Grandmother is teaching me about the plants she uses for dyeing wool. We go on long walks to look for them. She teaches me about the different colors the plants produce. When we return home, she cooks each plant in a pot of water. She adds a little bit of her own urine to the pot to keep the colors from fading over time.

"Late last spring, Marshall took me to the Red Rock community sheep shearing event in a very large corral where many men and women gathered to help each other shear the sheep. A huge amount of wool came off each of the Churro sheep. They looked naked after it was over.

"Marshall encouraged me to try shearing one of the sheep. I didn't know how difficult it was to get every last bit of wool off the sheep without injuring the animal with the handmade shears. I accidentally cut my sheep's ear and made it bleed. I felt really sorry I hurt the animal. But no one paid much attention; they just went on with their work.

"By the time I finished shearing my one sheep, everyone else had already finished shearing all of their sheep and were making preparations to have a big community feast together. My right hand ached and the muscles in my forearm went into a spasm. I left the event with great admiration for the people's sheep-shearing skills.

"Back home, Grandmother and I carded the wool and then spun it. With our right hands, we rolled the drop spindle back and forth against our thighs, while our left hands held the wool that we spun into yarn.

"Grandmother washed the bundles of yarn in the water at the windmill. Now the yarn is ready to be dyed, or just left as it is and woven with its natural colors. Grandmother used to do a lot of weaving. I've seen her rugs—they're beautiful. Now she says she's getting old and doesn't have the energy to weave as much as she did when she was younger.

"Morris built me a loom that's attached to one of the poles outside so that I could finish the rug I started in Chinle. I have woven quite a few Navajo rugs so far. It's a form of relaxation for me. Here in Red Rock, I'm involved in the entire process of weaving a rug—herding the sheep, shearing them, carding the wool, spinning it with the old-fashioned drop spindle, harvesting and boiling the plants, dyeing the yarn, and then finally weaving the rug. When I see a well-made Navajo rug, I feel a deep admiration for all the work involved.

"I'm working on a new rug now. It's long and narrow, with an intricate Navajo pattern. I love to weave, even though my legs go numb from sitting cross-legged for more than an hour. Weaving takes a lot of time and work. I have spun all my own wool. The spinning takes me as much time as the weaving itself.

My loom is tied onto the front of the tree.
Grandmother's is tied to the back.

Weaving is an opportunity to rest without being criticized. If I just lie down and do nothing while resting, Grandmother starts telling anyone who will listen, '*t'oo seti*,' meaning, 'she's just sitting around.'

"Grandmother just finished weaving a rug herself. It's a saddle blanket for her horse. It's not an especially fancy rug, but it's still a fine piece of work, made mostly of old scraps of yarn that she wanted to use up. I'm amazed at how well Grandmother still weaves in her eighties."

Morris prepares the loom for Virginia Tome.

August 15, 1973

"At this moment I am sitting inside the cabin on one of the beds, taking advantage of my time alone. Under Grandmother's bed is a box containing all sorts of little items she keeps hidden away, like the miniature leather pouches of corn pollen she uses for prayers. I wish I could look inside that box to see her secret things. I don't dare, though, because she'd probably figure out what I'd done and get after me.

"Above my bed is a rifle. Lee Tome told me I had to carry a gun when I herded sheep so that I could kill any coyotes I saw. I carried around the rifle for a few days, and then I put it back on the rack above my bed. I saw a few coyotes hanging around the corrals in the evening, but I let the dogs scare them off.

"I have to go take out the sheep. I'll talk to you tomorrow."

August 16, 1973

"I'm back. I'm on my horse, Jimmy, riding in back of the herd. The wind is blowing hard. It's five in the morning. The sheep are fat now and I am proud of it. Each sheep has a 'Q' on its rump, Lee Tome's brand.

"Lee Tome controls the breeding of his animals so that it happens only in the spring when the weather is warmer. Together we separated the rams and billy goats from the rest of the herd and put what looks like an apron around their middle, tied with a piece of string. The rubber apron hangs down, covering the animals' penises so that they won't impregnate any of the females.

"The rams and billy goats that Lee Tome has specially selected for breeding have huge balls that hang down between their hind legs, making it difficult for them to run because they swing back and forth.

"The females are in heat right now. The males that have not been castrated are constantly climbing on top of the females, even though they have on their apron condoms.

"Two rams are fighting just now as I am speaking. One ram taunts the other ram by kicking him. Then they square off and charge, butting their heads together, making a loud noise. Lee Tome says the rams and billy goats fight a lot during mating season.

115

"We've arrived at the windmill now. I just turned on the water and am waiting for the sheep to come and drink."

August 16, 1973

"A couple days ago, I took Grandmother over to the community branding near the trading post at Red Rock. All the people in the area get together and help brand the colts, the calves, and any cattle that haven't been branded yet. It's a fun and exciting time. The people gossip and catch up on the news. The women cook. A tribal official came to give the vaccinations to the cattle so they can qualify to be sold off the reservation at regular meat markets.

"The cowboys heat the branding irons in the fire until they are red hot. Then they press the hot irons against the flesh of the animal until it burns. They have to be careful not to leave the branding iron on too long, or the skin will become infected.

"When a big animal needs to be branded, the cowboys rope the head first, then the feet. They stretch the animal until it falls down. Then they pin it down while another cowboy brands the animal."

August 17, 1973

"One time I was herding sheep with Lee Tome's stud, riding bareback. I wanted to give him some exercise because he had been cooped up in the corral for several days. We were going over a hill. Just as we got to the other side, I saw Weemie's stud. He came charging toward my horse. I was petrified. Jimmy started stamping the ground, taking on a fighting stance with every muscle tense underneath my legs. Then he reared into the air. I had a hard time keeping from sliding off his rump. I held on tightly to his mane and somehow managed to stay on and turn him around. I got out of there as fast as I could. Weemie's stud chased us. I yelled at him, trying to sound ferocious. I finally managed to scare him off.

"Lately, I've been having long talks with Jimmy about life, what it means, and our purpose for being here. I think I'm getting closer to finding the purpose of my life, but I still don't know exactly what it is. I think it might have something to do with helping people. But how? I don't know. Jimmy has no opinion and just listens patiently. He's a good therapist.

I spent hours baring my soul to Jimmy while he listened in silence.

August 18, 1973

"Yesterday I received the biggest compliment ever from Virginia Tome and her relative, Sadie. After I cooked a big meal totally in the Navajo style with fried potatoes, fried chicken, and fry bread—using a lot of grease—they commented that I was almost ready for a man now.

"Sometimes I think they forget that I'm white. Sometimes I forget that myself."

CHAPTER 13
Walking in Another's Shoes

August 20, 1973

"I'm herding the sheep right now while I'm talking into the tape recorder. There's plenty of time out here in Red Rock to think about life.

"I am learning a lot about the Navajo way of being, acting, and thinking. Many things are becoming clearer to me, things I just couldn't understand in the beginning. When I first came to the reservation, I had a simplistic view that there was no basic difference between Navajos and Anglos. After all, both groups are humans struggling for survival on this earth. Both need food and shelter and human companionship. But after making countless cross-cultural blunders, I discovered that there are deep and fundamental differences in our beliefs and attitudes. These differences can be the cause of much misunderstanding.

"My feelings used to get hurt because the Navajo form of teasing seemed cruel. Now I realize it is one of the ways that the people show affection. Another thing that used to bother me was when I made every effort to do something for my Navajo friends to make them happy. No one expressed any gratitude. Finally I came to understand that traditional

Navajos say 'thank you' only after they receive some enormous favor. And no one says 'please' unless they are close to begging. When my Navajo friends ask for something, they say 'give me this,' instead of saying 'would you please give me this.' At first I thought it sounded bossy and demanding. Then I realized that in the Navajo language there is no other way to ask for something. Besides, the refinements of the English language seem out of place in this rugged environment.

"I am beginning to understand now how Navajo people might feel when they go off the reservation into the city to find employment. I bet they feel unappreciated and that their talents are disregarded or overlooked. I am in the same situation in reverse, something you rarely find—a person from the dominant culture becoming part of the minority culture. Right now I am the one who is feeling unappreciated and misunderstood. This experience has given me a lot of empathy and compassion for Navajos who live off the reservation.

"A few weeks after I came to Red Rock to herd sheep, I drove to Shiprock on my day off and bought four bags of groceries. I cooked a big, fancy dinner for Virginia and Lee Tome and Morris. I made them some of my favorite recipes as a special treat. They thought my cooking was no good and hardly ate any of the food I made—until I learned to cook Navajo food in their style. Now, looking back, I can see the humor in my misguided attempts to please them.

"Grandmother talks about me a lot. I don't understand every word she says, but I understand enough to know that she is very critical of the way I do things—the white man's way. I began to feel paranoid that she is talking about me all the time. I wonder if this is what Navajos who don't speak English feel like when they leave the reservation.

"Grandmother thinks I am ignorant when I can't do things the way she does them. When I first tried to make fry bread, she was impatient with me that I couldn't make the dough come out big and round and thin, like the way she makes it. It was hard to master the technique of slapping around that little ball of dough from one hand to the other, pulling the dough and shaping it all the while until it becomes perfectly round and thin, the size of a dinner plate.

"Grandmother is strict and critical because she expects from me the same behavior she would from a Navajo woman. I'm convinced she's trying to prepare me to be Marshall's wife."

I shared all these feelings with Marshall when he showed up one Saturday. We took a walk together among the red rocks a little ways west of the cabin. He listened and then said in a gentle, kind voice that I was being overly worried and that his mother liked me a lot. He pointed out that the Navajo language can sound rough and unfriendly to an English speaker.

Marshall reminded me that when I first arrived on the reservation, I thought that all the Navajo people were angry at each other because of the tone of their voices. Once I started learning the language, I realized that the guttural tones and glottal stops made the words sound harsh, even if they were friendly words.

Marshall said his mother told him that I was a good sheepherder and that she wanted me to stay with her in Red Rock. Marshall advised me not to worry about his mother wanting me to marry him. He reassured me that he would speak to her again and explain that I was not looking for a husband.

August 25, 1973

"I told Marshall that I was starting to think about life after teaching school and herding sheep. I told him I was searching for my purpose in life. He got very quiet, and then he leaned over and hugged me in a fatherly way and patted the top of my head, similar to the way I pat the sheep dogs when no one is looking. The touch felt good.

"We sat in silence until the moon came up, and then we walked back to the cabin. Marshall held my hand as we walked. My Navajo friends don't like to talk about their feelings, but I knew Marshall felt sad. I felt sad too. I have grown very fond of him.

"I'm starting to feel chilled sitting here among the rocks, watching the sheep and talking into the tape recorder. It looks like it is going to rain soon. Giant clouds are forming over the mountains. They are black with rain droplets.

"When it rains it's an exquisite sight to behold. The rain comes sweeping across the desert like a curtain blown by the wind. The weather can be dramatic and violent. The long grasses bend over and almost touch the ground. The rain makes a lot of noise as it strikes the ground.

"One time I got caught in a very violent rainstorm, too far from home to find shelter. I was completely drenched for a long time in the chilly air. When it rains hard like that, Jimmy puts his back to the rain. The sheep do the same as they huddle together."

August 26, 1973

"I finally learned how to use the sheep herding dogs effectively. In the beginning I didn't know what commands to use to make them round up the sheep. I made up my own commands and finally found a few that really work. For example, when I want the dogs to round up the sheep, I just start making gruff guttural sounds and point in the direction where I want them to gather the sheep. They actually understand. Several times when I heard Grandmother yell 'shaa dee,' the dogs ran away. Since Navajo/English dictionaries don't exist yet—as far as I know—I have to guess the meaning of the Navajo words that I hear. I assumed that 'shaa dee' means 'scram' or 'get out of here.' So when I want the dogs to leave the sheep alone, I just yell 'shaa dee.' It works.

"There is an art to sheep herding. It is not quite as simple as it appears. Before I learned the art, it was one frustration after another. I yelled at the sheep when they got too far behind the rest of the herd because they would lose their way and run off in all directions. That was before I learned the trick of turning around the whole herd to meet up with the stragglers.

Sometimes a sheep will feel sick and lag far behind the rest. It needs constant prodding so it won't get so far behind that it gets lost.

"Sheep don't seem to have much brainpower. I have seen young sheep cry out for their mothers in a panic while the mother sheep are just a few feet away. They can get completely lost even when the rest of the herd is close by and making a lot of noise. Sometimes when I clear out the animals from the corral in the morning, the sheep will race around and around past the open gate, trying to find the way out when it is right in front of them.

"Goats are much more intelligent than sheep and never get lost. In fact, the goats act like leaders, making sure the herd heads in the right direction.

Sheep and goats returning to their corrals

"Some of the sheep and goats wear bells around their necks. The tinkling bells remind me of my times in Switzerland visiting my relatives.

"When the goat kids get a little bigger and don't need so much milk, I'm going to separate the mothers from the babies for one night. In the morning I'll milk the mothers and get some goat milk to drink. There's often not enough milk to drink around here. I want to use it on my oatmeal."

August 27, 1973

"Spending so much time on Jimmy's back, I've gotten pretty good at roping. I usually carry a rope with me, attached to the saddle, while I am herding sheep. Sometimes when I have nothing to do, I dismount Jimmy and rope the saddle horn. I avoid roping the sheep and goats. I don't want the rope to land on them and cause a stampede.

"I do all sorts of tricks with Jimmy to pass the time. I practice trying to get onto his back by vaulting myself from behind. First I let Jimmy know what I'm about to do by placing my hand on his rump and then running my hand down his thigh. I walk a ways away, and then I run at full speed toward him. I put my hands on Jimmy's rump and spring up like a frog. Thankfully, he knows to remain motionless as I try out my tricks. I have never made it all the way onto his back—not even once. But I keep trying. Jimmy is very tall.

"I also practice getting on without a saddle. I hold onto Jimmy's mane and swing my leg up and over his back. I've watched the cowboys do these tricks in the rodeos. I also practice standing on Jimmy's back in my bare feet. It's hard to keep my balance when he's walking. When the sheep are not moving too much and just calmly eating, I lie on Jimmy's back and stare at the sky.

I would take the sheep out early in the morning before the sun rose.

"I'm riding Jimmy as I speak. He is quite a character. Smart too. We get along well. He used to be wild. Grandmother was the only one who could ride him. He has herded sheep for so long that he is tame now. When I first rode him, he was angry. He put his ears flat against his neck and tried to bite me. Now he trusts me. When I go out to saddle him up in the morning, he walks over to me and gives me a whinny and then nuzzles me.

"When I saddle him, he tricks me by swelling up his belly so I won't make the cinch strap too tight. After a few minutes, he lets out the air. At first I was fooled. I would lead him out of the corral and tie him to a post while I took out the sheep. Then, when it was time to get on him,

I would put my foot in the stirrup, reach up for the saddle horn, heave myself up—and fall flat on my back with the saddle sliding down to his underside. Now I check the cinch before I get on. If I accidentally make the cinch too tight, Jimmy reaches around and tries to bite me.

"When I'm out riding, he wants to stop and eat all the time. But I have him trained now so that the only time he eats is when I say 'whoa Jimmy, whoa.' (When I said that just now into the recorder, he thought I was talking to him and stopped to eat.) Sometimes he pretends he has to pee just so I will loosen up on the reins. He'll stretch out his legs in the position that horses take when they pee. But instead of peeing, he'll reach down and start eating. Now I am wise to his tricks. He doesn't get away with it anymore. I admire his cleverness.

August 28, 1973

"Marshall brought his children, Desbah and Deswood, for another visit while I was living in Red Rock. I enjoyed watching them enthusiastically explore their surroundings. When they spotted Jimmy, they wanted to ride him and help with the sheep herding. When both kids climbed onto Jimmy's back, he wouldn't budge. They called me over and asked me to help move him. I took the reins and pulled him. What I did must have been painful, because he reared up and kicked with his front legs. Then I realized that the kids had put his bridle on backwards! His show of force impressed me. He is usually docile, just walking around in the desert, herding the sheep with me.

August 29, 1973

"When I first arrived the end of May, there were quite a few desert wildflowers. The blossoms are the favorite food of the sheep and goats. They're gone now.

"The sheep and goats just eat and eat. They poop while they are eating. It seems like a constant stream of feces is coming out of them.

"Most of the sheep and goats have their ears clipped. This is a form of branding. Some have tags to identify who owns them in the family. Many of these sheep and goats have been given to the grandchildren and other relatives, but they are all kept together with the main herd. The relatives are allowed to come and claim them for butchering whenever they want.

"I have to bring the sheep in now. I'll be right back with you soon."

"I'm under the shade house now. Lee and Virginia Tome have gone to the Chapter House for the Sunday meeting. They went over to talk about the dispute they are having with Weemie and his horse, who likes to fight with Lee Tome's stud. Their son Harry is a councilman for this district.

"This must be the season for bugs. Outside it's swarming with gnats, making life uncomfortable. When I am herding sheep, they fly around my face and try to get in my eyes and nose. I just now blew my nose and three came out.

"At home under the shade house, the place is swarming with flies. When I'm weaving, they land on my body. If I don't swat them quickly, they bite. The two ducks and three geese eat the dead flies off the ground. I discovered that if I rub my body with the leaves of the sagebrush plant, the insects leave me alone. I think the odor is too pungent for them.

"Since no one is home and we are out of water, I put the barrels in the truck and went to the artesian well, where water comes out of the ground through a pipe. After filling the barrels, I went home and unloaded them. They're very heavy. It was hard work. No wonder they are so sparing of water.

"I'm very impressed by the resourcefulness of the people out here. When they don't have something that is absolutely essential, they find a way to get by with what they have. For example, if Grandmother needs string, she spins it herself. And it's amazing the many uses for the rubber from old tires and pieces of wire—like for fixing the fence posts in the corral and for repairing their tools. Virginia and Lee Tome seem to be able to mend just about anything."

September 1, 1973

"Today I have been here three months. Lately, while I'm out with the sheep, I've been spending a lot of time daydreaming about where I will go after my summer herding sheep ends and what direction my life will take. I want to explore the world and learn about other cultures. I remember Vreni talking to me enthusiastically about the Peace Corps when she worked in their main office in Washington, D.C. for a few months."

CHAPTER 14

Goodbye for Now

September 3, 1973

"I'm sitting on the ground with my legs stretched out and my back against a warm rock, talking to you on the tape recorder. The sun is about to set right behind me. I'm alone. It's quiet and peaceful. I have some thoughts and feelings I want to share with you.

"I've been out here herding sheep all summer with lots of solitude and time to think about life while I'm riding around on Jimmy's back.

"I could stay in Red Rock forever, marry Marshall, and become a certified member of the Navajo Tribe—and hope you all would come visit me out here once in a while. But I can't do that. I'm too young to settle down. I have a deep yearning to explore the world and find my purpose.

"When I first came to the reservation, I wanted to turn around and go home. If Daddy hadn't told me that I shouldn't judge anybody or anything on first appearances and that I should give the Navajo Reservation a three-month trial before quitting, I might have missed out on one of the most important experiences of my life. And who knows what direction my life would have taken at that point.

"Wait—I have to turn off the recorder. I get choked up when I talk about all this.

"I'm back. So, in the face of what I just said, it will probably sound crazy what I'm about to tell you.

"I've been thinking about joining the Peace Corps and working with the Indians in South America. But when I think about leaving Red Rock and the Navajo People, I feel really sad.

"I cherish the two powerfully life-changing years I've spent on the reservation. At the same time, I hunger to learn more about life in other parts of the world.

"I have the distinct feeling that if I don't leave the reservation right now at this juncture, then I probably will never leave, since I'm so attached to the people and their enchanting land.

"I'm going to walk back to the cabin and get ready for bed. It's almost dark. I'll talk to you tomorrow."

September 5, 1973

"Since I last talked to you, I've been digesting a sad and painful encounter.

"Yesterday evening, when we were sitting in the shade house watching the night roll in, I told Virginia and Lee Tome that I was going to leave the reservation in a week or two.

"Grandmother asked, 'Where are you going?'

"I answered, 'I am going home.'

"She said firmly, 'Your home is here on the reservation.'

"'But, I mean home to my mother and father,' I said.

"There was a long, uncomfortable silence.

"Finally Lee Tome asked, 'Where do they live?'

"'In New England,' I said.

"'Where is New England?' Lee Tome stumbled over the pronunciation of the two strange English words.

"I answered, 'Next to the big water, where the sun rises in the east.'

"There was another very long silence—maybe 15 minutes of silence—while Lee Tome smoked his hand-rolled cigarette and Grandmother looked out into the darkness.

"'When will you come back?' Grandmother asked, breaking the silence.

"My voice quivered, 'I don't know.'

"No one said a word the rest of the evening. Oh God. I feel so ripped up inside.

"In a way, the reservation really is a kind of home for me—a spiritual home. Part of my heart will always remain here.

"It's odd the way my Navajo friends have never asked me about my life before I came to the reservation. It's as though my life didn't exist until I started living with the Navajo people. So when I talk about wanting to go home, they respond with surprise and incomprehension.

"I'm in my car right now, driving back from Chinle. I went there to pack up my things, tie up some loose ends, and say goodbye to my friends—including Donna and Juanita and a few of my students that I happened to see in town.

"When I told the principal of the boarding school that I would not be returning to teach in the fall, he was not surprised. He had assumed I would eventually leave to pursue advanced studies off the reservation.

"Oh shoot! I've used up the ten blank cassette tapes I brought with me to Red Rock. This last one has about one more minute left. I'll end here. See you soon. Bye for now. Over and out!"

I made two phone calls while I was in Chinle—one to Marshall and one to my older sister, Vreni, who lived in southern California. Marshall had been expecting to hear that I would be leaving the reservation. He admitted that he felt sad, but he knew we would be friends for life—and he was right about that.

Vreni and I had been writing letters back and forth since I left her place two years before and headed off to Chinle. She had visited me several times while I was teaching school. I told her about my plans and how hard it was for me to leave. She said she would like to come out and spend my final days on the reservation with me, and then we could leave together.

I drove to Albuquerque to pick Vreni up at the airport. I was happy to have her with me for those last bittersweet days in Red Rock. She boosted my morale. I shared with her my day-to-day life, including herding sheep.

"Wow! I had no idea you lived in such a stunningly beautiful place." Vreni was enthusiastic about being in Navajo country. She seemed to love every minute of her few days with me. We herded sheep together. She rode Jimmy while I rode Lee Tome's stud. While we passed the time watching the sheep and goats, Vreni quizzed me with endless curiosity about every aspect of life with Virginia and Lee Tome and the sheep.

While Vreni slept soundly in her sleeping bag on the sheepskins, I took the sheep out by myself one last time at five in the morning on the day of our departure.

On that last day, when I said good-bye to Lee Tome, he stretched out his hand and shook my hand firmly—the way white men shake hands when they're closing a business deal—and said *"Ahehe,"* meaning "thank you."

He opened his wallet and took out five $20 bills and handed them to me as the last month's payment for herding sheep. Then he turned around and went into the cabin and brought out a cloth bundle. He untied the bundle on the table in the shade house.

Two pieces of antique Navajo jewelry lay on the cloth—a long silver squash-blossom necklace and a beaded greenish-turquoise choker necklace. For nearly 40 years after leaving the reservation, I wore the greenish-turquoise beads around my neck every day, sometimes even to bed with me at night. I still wear them, but not every single day.

I walked over to Grandmother and reached out my hand to her. She gave me a typical Navajo handshake, meaning that her hand was almost limp in mine. She gave a barely perceptible squeeze to my hand and then our hands parted. She looked away and mumbled *"doo baa ii,"* along with some other Navajo phrases that let me know she wasn't happy that I was leaving.

I told Grandmother I would see her again one day. As I started to turn away, I saw her reach for a dark object on the outside table. It was the mysterious box that she kept under her bed. She opened the box and pulled out a leather pouch with corn pollen in it and handed it to me. Grandmother said I needed the corn pollen for when I pray to the Great Spirit to guide me and give me strength.

I felt like hugging her, but I didn't dare, since it would have been shocking for a traditional Navajo to receive an exuberant Anglo hug.

I turned to say goodbye to Morris. He kept his eyes looking down as he gave me a Navajo handshake, much like the handshake his mother had given me. He mumbled something in Navajo that was inaudible.

On that last day when Vreni and I drove down the dirt road toward the highway, I had to wipe away the tears that quietly rolled down my cheeks. Why was I leaving this place where I had been so happy and full of life, and where my spirit had been profoundly stirred?

I saw this view of Shiprock for the last time as my sister and I drove away from Virginia and Lee Tome's farm in Red Rock.

As we neared the highway, I had a strong intuition that someday I would return to the Navajo people in a different capacity. I had a debt of gratitude to repay the tribe for having accepted me into their lives and hearts.

Vreni and I spent the night in Gallup, New Mexico, and then left Navajo country and headed to Albuquerque. Vreni flew back to California the next day.

I stayed in Albuquerque for a few days to get myself oriented before embarking on the long road trip across the country to my parents' home in New Hampshire.

I wandered around aimlessly in Albuquerque's Old Town with an overwhelming sense of grief and loss. I needed to find an outlet for the emotions that I could barely contain in my body.

Without knowing exactly what I was doing, I went to an art supply store and bought a wooden circular frame and some glue. After I left the store, I rifled through the belongings stuffed in the back of my Bronco. I found a piece of black cowhide, some strips of leather, and a hunting knife that a friend had given me as a going-away gift.

Allowing an intuitive part of myself to take the reins, I created an image of a broken drum with the stretched cowhide, which I tore and then partially stitched together with the strips of leather. The basic circular frame remained intact. I pulled out three carefully wrapped eagle feathers from my suitcase—a sacred gift from a medicine man— and attached them to the torn drum. Although I could not articulate the symbolic meaning of my creation, it served to hold my grief so that I could breathe again.

The next day, I left Albuquerque and headed home. On the way out of town I found a pay phone and called Marshall. I told him that even though I didn't know what my future held, I knew with certainty that I'd be coming back to his people someday.

This creation was an expression of my feelings of love, gratitude,
grief, and loss on leaving the reservation and the Navajo people.

CHAPTER 15

The Peace Corps

New England and Ecuador, 1974–1976

Soon after I arrived at my parents' home, Marshall came to New Hampshire to visit me. He had planned on staying a week. My parents liked him immediately and treated him with warmth. Nevertheless, after two days in New England, he was ready to go back home to the reservation. I could sense his discomfort. I asked him privately why he wanted to leave early. His short response spoke volumes. "The sky is too small here." I knew exactly what he meant. The sky was too small for me, too.

I drove Marshall to the airport in Boston. We hugged each other at the gate. We both cried as we said goodbye. On the drive back home, I realized that I had never seen a Navajo man cry before—or hug in public.

My room on the third floor of my parents' house became like a museum of my life with the Navajos. Native American art objects filled the room from floor to ceiling, including all the shelves and dresser drawers. I hung my Navajo rugs—the ones I wove, bought, and received as gifts—on every wall. When I ran out of space, I carefully folded the rest of the rugs and stacked them neatly in a big pile on the spare bed.

My parents' home in New Hampshire

My parents lived in an historic, 200-year-old home. Although they rarely went up to the third floor, they did walk up the steep flight of stairs two or three times while I was home. They sat entranced among all the objects that represented my life with the Navajos. I gave them an abbreviated version of the story behind each piece.

All my treasures stayed in that room on the third floor while I followed my dream to serve in the Peace Corps. I had been assigned to a region high in the Andes Mountains of Ecuador to teach reading and writing to the Quechua-speaking Indians, direct descendants of the Incas.

The Peace Corps officials recognized that I had already been trained in bilingual education on the Navajo reservation. And they knew I spoke Spanish because I had spent six months in San Miguel de Allende, Mexico, studying art as part of my college education. They wanted me to use those skills to help the Indigenous people learn Spanish so that their children could eventually find work and help support their families.

The Peace Corps allowed me to choose my site where I would carry out my work assignment. I chose a remote village high in the Andes, near spectacular snow-covered peaks.

The bus from Quito dropped me off at a trailhead a few kilometers from the nearest town of Ambato. I hiked up the steep mountain with great excitement and anticipation—and a touch of fear of what I might encounter. I wore blue jeans, a bulky sweater to protect against the cold mountain air, and a pair of sturdy hiking boots. The heavy pack on my back measured more than half my height and extended above my head. It contained much of what I would need for the next two years during my stay in the tiny village nestled at 12,000 feet on the flanks of a huge mountain.

When I finally reached the remote Andean village of La Compañia de Jesus Cristo, the people fled at the sight of me. The Indians had hardly ever seen white people before—other than the Quechua-speaking priest from Spain who had lived among them for a few decades and had converted most of them to Catholicism.

In all those years, the priest never taught the Indians to read or speak Spanish with any proficiency. I assumed that the custom to keep the Indians illiterate was so they wouldn't have access to the Bible, where they could read for themselves what Jesus had to say.

My arrival in the mountain village overlapped with the priest's departure back to Spain. I got to spend a few days with him in his little house adjacent to the run-down chapel before his last hike down the mountain. Although he had never heard of the Peace Corps, he expressed suspicions that the organization had sent me to the village to instigate dissent among poor people and start a revolution. His parting words to me, spoken with gravitas, were, "Don't talk to the Indians about politics. They are simple. They don't understand these things. Don't pollute their minds."

A few decades earlier, an anthropologist had come to study the Indians. Rumor had it that the villagers killed him because they were afraid of him. But now they were good Catholics, and they weren't supposed to kill uninvited outsiders. At least, that's what I was counting on.

For the first few days, no one came near me. When I approached the people working in the fields, they dropped their hoes and fled to their thatch-roofed mud-brick homes. Even the dogs bolted away from me with their tails between their legs. I felt as alone as I ever had.

In my solitude, I took long walks. I noted that the surrounding fields produced quinoa, cabbage, and potatoes—the staples for the villagers' daily meals. For festive occasions, like a wedding or a saint's day, they killed and ate the guinea pigs that they kept on the dirt floors inside their homes. For those same celebrations, they made a strong alcoholic drink, called *chicha*, from the juice of yucca plants that grew along the dirt paths.

I wondered if the villagers had ever tasted fresh fruit. I remembered how much the Navajo children in my classroom loved eating the fruit I brought them.

One day I hiked down the mountain with my empty backpack. Once I made it to the paved road below, I hitched a ride to the nearest food market. I filled my pack with oranges and the staples I needed to cook meals in my makeshift kitchen—one of the few rooms that had an intact roof overhead in the half-collapsed hacienda ruin that I called home.

The long-abandoned, rat-infested stone and wood structure belonged to an absentee landowner in Quito who had given me permission to use his family's hacienda during my two-year assignment. He was convinced that I wouldn't last more than a couple of days living a life of "isolation and deprivation with the Indians."

After five hours of breathlessly lugging my heavy pack up the mountain, I finally arrived back at the village. While most of the villagers ran and hid, a few brave children stood their ground and looked at me with curiosity. They followed me to the hacienda, cautiously maintaining a safe distance behind me. When I got to the ramshackle building, I took the oranges out of my pack and held them in the air for the children to see. They inched a little closer to get a better look.

I placed an orange on the ground about 50 feet from the house and walked away. The children waited a few moments, and then ran toward the orange and stared at it. One of the children grabbed the orange and ran away. The rest of the kids trailed behind. The next day, I placed another orange on the ground and stood 20 feet away, waiting for the children to approach and grab the orange. Each day I placed one of the oranges a little closer to me.

By the fifth day, I held an orange in my outstretched hand. The children cautiously approached. About a dozen boys and girls encircled me. They were barefoot, with ragged and torn clothes. Their bright faces, full of curiosity, were framed by thick, jet-black hair. The boys wore pants and ponchos; the girls wore blouses, shawls hand-woven in bright colors, and dark skirts held up by woven waistbands. They smelled of wood smoke. One of the girls walked boldly up to me, grabbed the orange, and took off running.

The next day, the same girl approached where I sat on the stone steps of the hacienda. She looked at the orange in my hand and then looked fleetingly into my eyes. She slowly and cautiously climbed into my lap. After squirming around getting comfortable, she took the orange from my hand, placed it between her teeth, and bit out a piece of the rind. Then she squeezed the orange. The juice ran down her smiling face. As she began peeling the rind, some of the other children, mostly girls, drew closer and started cautiously touching me, as though I were a strange insect or a snake.

Most of the boys hung back as the girls explored my body. One of the girls touched my brown hair and ran a strand through her fingers, while another girl parted my hair with her fingers and peered in toward my scalp, probably looking for lice. A third girl gently rubbed the skin on my arm, as though checking to see if the white color would rub off.

The girls ran their hands over much of my body, poking and pinching my skin. The girl in my lap began patting my body, including my chest. When her hands touched my breasts, she screeched, "Mama!"

Her revelation resulted in a chorus of squeals echoing her discovery. After a few moments of motionless amazement, two of the girls reached over to see if it was really true that I was indeed a woman. All the children had big smiles on their faces as they ran home to spread the news.

It was understandable that the people had thought I was a man. In the Quechua culture, men wear pants and women wear skirts. I had brought only pants with me and, to make matters even more confusing for the villagers, my bulky sweater hid other clues they might have obtained regarding my gender. My shoulder-length hair offered no clues either, because both men and women wore long hair. And since I didn't speak much, they couldn't hear that my voice was definitely that of a woman.

Most puzzling of all for them was that I traveled alone. Within the Quechua culture, no woman would ever venture far beyond her home without a man to accompany her.

Now that the children had discovered my gender, word spread throughout the village. From that moment on, the community no longer saw me as a potential threat, and they accepted me into their lives.

Every morning, the children came to ask for fruit. One day I pulled out one of my cameras, a Polaroid, to take a picture of them. Before I could press the button, they fled in terror.

A few days later, one of the braver boys agreed to hold the camera in his hands. I showed him how to take a picture of his friends. When the children saw the developed photograph, they couldn't understand what they were seeing. They turned the picture around in all directions, trying to make sense out of the shapes on the piece of paper. Finally, one of the girls pointed to a boy in the photo and then pointed to the boy that matched the image. The children gasped in unison.

Over time, all the kids wanted their picture taken. The adults, on the other hand, wouldn't have anything to do with being photographed. They were convinced that the camera would capture their spirit, much like what the traditional Navajos believed would happen.

I had learned a little Quechua before taking on this assignment, but not much—enough to make myself understood when supplemented with gestures and mime.

After a couple of weeks, I played a new game with the children. In order for them to get their piece of fruit, they each needed to tell me a little story in Quechua that I would record with my portable tape recorder, a little black box that did not frighten them because it looked a lot like the little black Instamatic camera that they had grown used to.

Most of the stories were simple descriptions of their lives on the mountain. When I played back the recordings, the children were mesmerized. They thought I was a magician who came from a mystical land far away. I told them I lived in a place called *North America*, words that didn't mean anything to them.

An itinerant Spanish-speaking teacher, Pilar, came every few weeks to the village and helped me transcribe and translate the children's stories into Spanish. We worked in the tiny, one-room schoolhouse near my hacienda. Eventually, we used the growing collection of transcribed stories to help the children learn to read. We intended to make a bilingual primer and an abbreviated bilingual dictionary that would be used in the Quechua-speaking schools in the remote mountain villages.

After a few weeks in the village, the adults wanted to get a closer look at the stranger from a faraway place called *North America*, where the people have magical powers and where women look and act like men.

The children relayed to me the invitations from their families to join them in a meal. Invariably, the meals consisted of a huge bowl of soup with everything they grew—quinoa, cabbage, onions, potatoes, and herbs. To honor me, the people sometimes killed one of their precious guinea pigs.

I had tried to revert back to being a vegetarian after I left the Navajo reservation, but I dropped that idea when the Peace Corps officials advised me and the other volunteers to make sure we did not offend our hosts. This meant we needed to eat the food that people offered us, including guinea pigs.

I gagged down the guinea pig meat, trying to appear like I was enjoying the taste. Actually, the taste wasn't bad—a bit like tender chicken. It was the idea of eating rodents that made me queasy.

During the home visits, the host or hostess would invariably ask me where my husband was. When I replied that I didn't have a husband, they laughed at the preposterous idea. They could not fathom a single woman roaming around the world on her own.

After each meal, I lingered for about an hour or so before returning home. During that time, the girls in the family came over and looked for lice on my head. I learned to relax and enjoy the lice inspections, knowing they were a form of socializing.

After a few weeks, the adults started lining up in front of the hacienda every morning, bringing me their problems. They insisted on calling me *Patrona*, the term for a woman boss. Each time I responded in my broken Quechua mixed with Spanish, "I'm not your boss. My name is Erica."

They answered, *"Si, Patrona."*

Each morning, villagers lined up in front of the hacienda, waiting for "Patrona" to appear.

Early one morning as I lay in bed, I heard a woman's voice yelling for help, *"Patrona. Patrona. Ayudenos!"*

I threw on my clothes and went to the entryway of the hacienda. I pushed aside the piece of cloth I used for a door and stepped outside. Three anxious mothers were holding crying babies who looked feverish and congested, bundled up tightly in shawls.

The mothers asked me to "cure the babies." I told them emphatically that I was not a doctor and did not know what to do. They responded, *"Si, Patrona."*

The mothers stood their ground, begging and pleading for me to do something. I repeated that I didn't know what to do because I was not a doctor.

I wanted with all my heart to help these mothers and their sick babies. I tried to hold back my tears.

Please God help me. What can I do?

After imploring help from the heavens, I went resolutely inside the hacienda, took out the first aid kit that the Peace Corps office had given me, found the bottle of aspirin, and took out one single tablet. I crushed the tablet with the handle of my knife until only a tiny pile of white dust remained.

I went outside and told the mothers that I had found some medicine. I went to each baby and placed a grain of the white dust on the baby's tongue. With two fingers, I made the sign of the cross on each baby's forehead, knowing that the Indians were Catholic, and then I said a short prayer in Spanish that I made up on the spot. The mothers smiled and walked away.

Although the mothers seemed pleased, I felt guilty—as though I had committed a mortal sin by impersonating a Catholic. And what good would come from pretending that a grain of aspirin would help them? I hoped God would forgive me for being an imposter.

The next morning I heard a women's voice outside, calling *"Patrona! Patrona!"* I ran to the front entry. Two of the mothers had returned, each holding a roasted guinea pig impaled on a stick from the anus to the mouth.

Before I could think about how I was going to eat those gifts, which looked a lot like skewered rats, my attention abruptly shifted back to the mothers. They told me in broken Spanish, "All three babies cured. Big miracle. May God pay you!" I asked them to repeat what they said a

145

second, then a third time to make sure that I understood exactly what they were saying. *"Si, Patrona, toditos guaguas curados. Milagro grande. Que Dios le pague."*

Oh my God. How is that possible? How can all three of those sick babies be cured? A speck of aspirin can't cure any illness. And the made-up prayer I recited in Spanish was incomprehensible to those mothers. They don't speak much Spanish, other than a few words and expressions.

I couldn't understand what happened. Then I remembered the miraculous healings I had witnessed with the Navajo people in the peyote ceremonies. I couldn't explain those miracles either.

Word spread around the region about the healing of the babies. People lined up to receive a "cure" from the Patrona. I went along with the charade, feeling that, at the very least, my care and concern couldn't hurt. Their regard for me did not seem to diminish when my cures didn't work—which was more often than not, especially with the adults.

But just the fact that my ministrations ever worked at all was mind-blowing to me. It wasn't until a few years after leaving the Peace Corps that I learned exactly what the placebo effect is and how it works with the immense power of the mind.

The pure faith of the mothers, relayed through some metaphysical connection with their sick babies, was able to change the babies' condition overnight. I've often wondered if my heartfelt desire to relieve the suffering of the mothers and their babies might have played a role in the healing as well.

Whatever the chain of cause and effect, I loved the taste of being able to help alleviate suffering. The seeds for becoming a doctor had gotten another big watering.

One of the little girls who liked to sit in my lap

I learned a lot from the Quechua-speaking Indians in the village. I learned how to live with practically no material possessions without feeling deprived in any way. The $120 a month that the Peace Corps paid me felt like a fortune and put me in a similar earning capacity as Ecuadorian lawyers and doctors of that era.

I learned that feeling poor was a relative experience. The Indians did not feel that they were poor because they had nobody to compare themselves to. If they had been exposed to television, I think they would have begun to feel unhappy with their lives. I asked a man who was more fluent in Spanish than the others if he was happy with his life. He said, *"Patrona*, I am not happy or sad. This is our life." I remembered the priest's words about not talking about politics and poverty.

During my stay on the mountain, I also learned some tricks for safe pest control. Through mime and scratching gestures, I conveyed to one of the children that insects—fleas, mosquitoes, and bed bugs—came into my bed at night and bit me. The young girl showed me how to take leaves from the eucalyptus trees that dotted the countryside, crush them in my hands, and then rub the leaves on my skin. She also told me to put some of the eucalyptus leaves under my bed. From then on, I had no more problems with insects.

My two-year assignment passed quickly. The villagers knew that I would leave and go back to the faraway place called North America at the end of two years. I had made that departure date very clear from the beginning.

I noticed that I felt more reserved with the Quechua-speaking Indians than with the Navajo people. And I made less of an all-out effort to learn Quechua and engage with the villagers on a deeper level. I wanted to avoid repeating the painful scene with my Navajo friends when I precipitously announced that I was leaving the reservation and going home—after they had wholeheartedly accepted me into their lives, their homes, and their sacred ceremonies.

The villagers planned a big party to send me off. They showed up in their freshly washed clothes at the large courtyard in front of the run-down hacienda. The men transported an enormous caldron of homemade *chicha* alcohol using wooden poles balanced on their shoulders. The women brought baskets of food, including roasted guinea pigs. A few of the men brought instruments to make music, including panpipes, flutes, a drum, and an instrument that looked like a mandolin.

When the men got sufficiently drunk, they began singing and dancing to the music. Some of the bolder women began dancing too. I joined in, even though I remained sober, having taken only a few sips of *chicha* to avoid being rude. The festivities lasted until the early morning. I went to bed long before the party ended.

A few days before my departure from Ecuador, I received news that a printing press in Quito had published our bilingual collection of stories, called *Nucunchimunda*, which translates as "All About Us." The book was used for about ten years in the little classrooms in the mountain villages of Ecuador, according to Pilar, the itinerant teacher whose daughter found me on Facebook four decades later.

I cashed in my return ticket to the States on Pan American Airways and spent the $600 traveling around the South American continent for seven months before returning home. During those travels, I had a chance to reflect more on the unfolding meaning and purpose of my life.

I observed that I had a great interest in learning about people who were different from me. I tried to see the world through their eyes so I could understand their feelings and motivations and develop a connection with them.

I also took note of the joy I felt when I could be of service to others and make a difference in their lives.

All the paths I had taken so far were leading me in a certain direction, preparing me for my ultimate purpose. Although I didn't know yet what that was, I knew I simply needed to follow my instincts, even if those instincts prompted me to go in a direction that didn't make any sense to those around me—and sometimes didn't make sense to me either.

CHAPTER 16

Back Home in the States

1976–1986

Two and a half years after leaving for South America, I returned to my parents' home in New Hampshire. When I entered my room on the third floor, I immediately noticed that something wasn't right. The Navajo rugs on the walls looked dirty. I touched one to brush off what looked like dust. The entire rug disintegrated into a cloud of debris made up of wool fibers, moth excrement, larvae, and live moths. I moved from one rug to the next in a state of horror. The entire room was infested. Every item made of wool was beyond salvage.

I collapsed onto my bed and cried. There was no one I could blame for this disaster—not even myself. I had no experience with moth infestations and I couldn't blame my parents, because they rarely climbed the stairs to the third floor.

I will never forget those rugs and all that went into them—herding and shearing the sheep, carding, spinning and dyeing the wool, and finally the weaving. When the tears stopped, my spirit filled with deep feelings of gratitude to the Navajo people and the precious gift they had given me by accepting me into their lives.

I spent the next day removing all the items made of wool. I wrapped them in a white sheet as though I were wrapping a dead body. I dug a hole and buried the remains of the rugs in the far corner of my parents' vast garden, near a wild berry patch. I sprinkled some corn pollen on the burial site and then said a prayer in Navajo.

To this day, when I see a clothes moth, I'm stirred with a dreadful sense of loss.

A few months after I returned from the Peace Corps, I moved to Colorado, where I taught mountaineering for Outward Bound during the summer. Having witnessed the profound impact that being in nature had on my students, I decided to get my master's degree in education and then open a school for outdoor education.

Shortly after returning to the West, I drove out to the Navajo reservation to visit Marshall. We had a warm, heartfelt reunion and reminisced together. I shared with him my experiences with the Indigenous people of Ecuador. After patiently listening while I told my many stories, he brought me up to date on the happenings around the reservation, including news about Virginia and Lee Tome's 70th anniversary celebration. I drove to Arizona to visit him several times while I lived in Colorado.

The coursework for my master's degree required very little time and effort, so I decided to sign up for a few science courses, like biology and biochemistry—subjects I longed to know more about. I hadn't taken those courses in college because I had tested out of the science and math requirements, thanks to my rigorous high school education in Germany.

I discovered that most of my young classmates in the advanced placement science courses were premedical students. While taking those courses, I had a surprising revelation. Unwittingly, I had stepped onto the path that would eventually lead me to fulfilling the purpose of my life.

Against all odds—no money, considered too old at 29, wrong gender, and wrong background with my liberal arts degree—I applied to the University of Colorado School of Medicine. To my surprise, the school not only accepted me, they offered me a generous scholarship that covered tuition for the first two years of medical school. The National Health Service Corps gave me a loan to cover the last two years. In return, I would provide medical care in an underserved area for two years after I finished my training.

During the last year of my residency training, I took time off to visit various sites around the country that qualified as "medically under-served" in order to fulfill my obligation with the National Health Service Corps.

One of the hospitals where I interviewed was the Indian Health Service hospital in Shiprock, New Mexico. After the interview, I spent the afternoon trying to find Virginia and Lee Tome's cabin.

The long, rutted dirt road to Red Rock had been paved, allowing me to reach that area in a fraction of the time it used to take. My heart pounded as I recognized the cabin, the ceremonial hogan, and the corrals. There was a newly built cinderblock house that Marshall had told me about. The property looked abandoned. I decided to walk around to indulge myself in some nostalgia.

I heard a familiar whinny. I went to the corrals and saw Jimmy up against the railing with his eyes focused on me! He looked just the same, even though by now he was old in horse years. He nuzzled against my chest. I slipped through the railing and put my arms around his neck and my cheek against his hair, breathing in his familiar smell. I could barely contain my emotions. It took all my willpower not to climb onto Jimmy's back and ride off into the sagebrush like the old days.

I walked over to the cinderblock house and opened the door. It was dark inside. A weak voice screeched *"Eee yaa,"* an exclamation of fright in Navajo. I peered into the dimly lit room. Virginia Tome sat in the far corner, shriveled up and ancient. She was about 98 years old. Her pupils showed the large white opacities of cataracts that had left her totally blind.

"Ya'at'eeh Shimá sání," I greeted her. ("Hello, my Grandmother.")

Without even pausing to ask my name, she replied, "So you have come back to herd sheep again."

"No, Grandmother, I am no longer a sheepherder," I answered.

I wanted to tell her that I was a doctor. Not having spoken Navajo in many years, I could not remember the word for *doctor*. So I improvised.

"I am a *Hatáli"* (a medicine man). She laughed, showing her toothless gums.

"Where is your man?" she asked.

"I have no man. I am not married," I replied.

Her response was a familiar one. *"Bilagáana, t'oo diigiiz."* (White people are really crazy.)

I waited in the cinderblock house, talking with Virginia Tome, until one of her adult grandkids came home. I got caught up some more on the family news and learned that Lee Tome had died when he was almost 100 years old.

During the long drive back to Colorado, my past life with the Navajo people flashed in front of me, filling me with nostalgia and gratitude, along with a vague sense of longing for something from long ago that was no longer there.

CHAPTER 17

Cuba, New Mexico

1986–1988

Cuba is located at the base of the Jemez Mountains, not far from magnificent wilderness country, full of bears, elk, mountain lions, and wild turkeys. The town itself has been described on more than one occasion as "godforsaken" by travelers passing through on their way to somewhere else. Shops, gas stations, and restaurants lined the road that runs through town, at that time a poorly maintained two-lane highway connecting Albuquerque to the south and Farmington to the north.

In those days, the town had only 2,500 inhabitants, but the clinic and little hospital also served thousands of people who lived within a 75-mile radius.

Tucked away in the surrounding high desert and mesas lived clusters of Navajo families, hardscrabble Anglo and Hispanic ranchers, and the many employees who worked at the Cuba Health Center—along with a sprinkling of Anglo artists and writers, renegades, and other eccentrics who had left mainstream America behind.

I came to Cuba fresh out of my residency in family practice at Mercy Medical Center in Denver, Colorado. I looked forward to repaying my loan with the National Health Service Corps by spending two years working in an underserved area. Throughout my medical training, I had an idealized image of myself spending the rest of my life as a rural doctor serving a Native American population.

Cuba, New Mexico, seemed like the ideal place, especially knowing that many of my patients would be Navajos. On my site visit, I met the Health Center's staff of doctors, physician assistants, emergency medical technicians, and nurses. The staff seemed bright and energetic. I could easily envision myself working with this team of dedicated and congenial healthcare providers. I enthusiastically signed the two-year contract to fulfill my National Health Service obligation.

A month before I would leave Colorado to begin my highly anticipated first job, one of the doctors from the Cuba Health Center, Leonard Cain, phoned me with some startling news.

"Erica, I feel compelled to let you know what you're getting yourself into by coming to the Cuba Health Center. It's not what it was when you came for your site visit last fall. Every single member of the crew of physicians you met during your visit quit their jobs last month in protest over the policies of Presbyterian Medical Services, the governing organization in Santa Fe."

He said that PMS had drastically cut back funding in the name of cost containment. Vitally important health programs had been either eliminated or scaled way back; the satellite clinics were in danger of closing. The medical staff had been frustrated with PMS policies for years, and this latest change was the last straw.

Dr. Cain closed with, "I'm really sorry to bring you this bad news. But it didn't seem fair that no one told you what you'd be facing when you came here. To put it bluntly, you'll be on your own. But at least you'll have help from the nurse practitioners, the PAs, and the EMTs, who are all highly competent. They'll be a big help to you and a source of valuable information. Often they have more experience than the new doctors. I'm sorry, Erica. All of us had been looking forward to working side by side with you. Good luck."

The news that I would be the only full-time doctor on staff, without the team of physician colleagues I had initially expected and looked forward to, left me feeling terribly disappointed and apprehensive about my new position at the Cuba Health Center.

How will I know what to do with no one around to help me—no supervising physicians to guide me? Can I handle all the work by myself? Oh my God! This is going to be a much greater challenge than I ever imagined.

Somehow, I survived that first night on duty at the Cuba Health Center—a night of one emergency after another, including the failed attempt at resuscitating a dead medicine man under primitive, third-world conditions. After I filled up on caffeine and sugar from the convenience store, the morning greeted me with a room full of patients waiting to be seen in the clinic.

Bill, the temporary fill-in doctor, arrived at eight o'clock, looking fresh and chipper. He'd obviously had a good night's sleep. "You wouldn't believe the night I had on call," I said.

"Oh, yes I would," Bill answered with certainty. Apparently my experience was not that unusual.

Staying alert during the many appointments that day proved to be challenging. The secretary had scheduled me to see patients about every ten minutes, just enough time to hear a three-minute history from the patient, give a two-minute exam, and take five minutes for writing out the prescriptions for pills and giving an explanation about how to take them.

It's no surprise that the Navajo word for a western doctor is *azee'iil'ini*, which means "the one who gives out pills." With sad resignation, I became the stereotypical pill dispenser. I could see no alternative, given the circumstances I had to work within.

Approximately 40 patients came to me for help that first day in the clinic. With the dozen or so patients that I had seen the night before, this meant I had treated nearly 60 patients in a 24-hour period—not an unusual experience for the Cuba Health Center, I would come to discover.

At the end of the day, around 5:30, I walked to my car in a daze, wondering if I could maintain this pace for two years.

I drove home into the foothills in the partially dried mud with my little Honda sedan sliding in the ruts, oblivious to the breathtaking beauty surrounding me. After unpacking a few boxes in my tiny adobe house, I succumbed to exhaustion. I was too tired to think about what I had gotten myself into in this remote part of New Mexico—and too tired to care about the sounds of mice scampering around the room.

When I reported to work the following morning at eight o'clock, I discovered that I was scheduled to be on call again that night. The thought of being on duty all night again, after seeing an endless stream of patients all day, was daunting. I hadn't even had time to recover from my first night on call.

Bill saw me staring in disbelief at the call schedule. He said, "We will alternate night duty and weekends until the administration in Santa Fe can persuade a few more temporary doctors like myself to provide some relief."

After looking at my call schedule more closely, I made some quick calculations. The average number of hours that I would spend on duty each week ranged from 90 to over 100.

These figures promised to take my understanding of sleep deprivation to a new level, even beyond the extreme deprivation I had already experienced during my internship.

My second night on call was fortunately less brutal than the first night, but was marked by more misadventures. An adolescent Navajo girl came to the emergency room doubled over with periodic waves of pain, saying she had appendicitis. She came alone. A family member had dropped her off and driven away. Marie was a heavy-set 14-year-old wearing a very large white T-shirt. On routine questioning, she denied being pregnant or ever having had sex.

I helped Marie climb onto the exam table and then I put on latex gloves for the abdominal and pelvic exam. Her abdomen felt rock hard. I lifted the drapes and saw a baby's head crowning in the vaginal canal.

"You don't have appendicitis. You are going to have a baby," I announced, trying not to sound shocked. Marie lay still on the bed as the tears rolled down her cheeks. During the difficult delivery, not a single sound came out of Marie's mouth—no screams, no moaning. After the delivery, the young girl remained mute. She did not answer my questions, just stared at the ground.

As soon as I spoke a few words to her in Navajo, she revealed to me, with her hands covering her face, that her uncle had raped her. I made arrangements for Social Services to come by in the morning. In the meantime, I gave her all the emotional comfort I could, given the limitations of the situation.

My tired heart ached for this young girl. I heard later from one of the Navajo staff members that Marie never bonded with her baby. She gave the baby to her auntie, who welcomed the new member of the family with great joy. Marie went back to school and got counseling through the school system. The uncle received no punishment for the rape.

During a lull in the action, I drove home to try to get a little rest before the next drama unfolded. I'd gotten about an hour of fitful sleep when the phone rang. The EMT on duty informed me that there was a woman in labor at the clinic and asked if I could come back to check her.

I jumped into my Honda and swerved down the heavily rutted road. Halfway to the clinic, my car got stuck in the thick, red mud, which covered the wheels and caked the sides. There were no cell phones in those days, and I didn't have the hospital's two-way radio with me. I got out of the car and ran the remaining two miles in the dark, hoping I wouldn't sprain my ankle in one of the ruts in the road.

By the time I reached the clinic, splattered with mud and out of breath, the nurse on duty had already delivered the baby. Fortunately, there were no complications. But the muddy jog had quickly converted me. My next free weekend off duty, I drove the 85 miles to Albuquerque and bought a blue Toyota four-wheel-drive pickup truck. From then on, I looked like I belonged in this part of the world—at least while I was driving the truck.

During another memorable night on call, I again tried to slip away to get a little sleep. It wasn't long before the phone rang. It was the EMT, saying I needed to come in right away to pronounce a car accident victim dead. I jumped out of bed and into my brand-new blue pickup truck and sped to the clinic.

"Why do I need to pronounce the victim dead when it is clear he is already dead? Can't this wait until morning?" I asked the bleary-eyed EMT. He answered, "Just routine protocol. It's for the death certificate."

The victim on the gurney had no head. A few miles outside of town, a tractor-trailer truck had accidentally driven over his small car, taking the top off the car and decapitating the driver. Looking at the headless man was a shocking and nauseating experience. Some deep, slow breathing kept me from fainting.

Despite the emotionally traumatic experiences and overwhelming fatigue, I realized that I was getting an incredible, once-in-a-lifetime, hands-on medical education in the trenches, an opportunity that few doctors ever have—for better or worse. Similar to how doctors work in a third-world setting, I was doing procedures that are normally done by specialists—not because I wanted to do these procedures, but because they needed to be done and no one else was around to do them on an emergency basis.

It was not uncommon for me to have an orthopedic medical textbook open next to the patient lying on the exam table in the emergency room with a dislocation or a compound fracture, or in need of a Bier block—a regional anesthetic technique normally administered by anesthesiologists. Given the circumstances, we had to manage on our own.

Referring to a textbook in front of the patient did not usually inspire confidence in them. Some of the Navajo patients thought they were serving as guinea pigs for the doctor's training and expressed resentment, a sentiment I could well understand. But most of the patients were grateful that they could get any help at all in this remote area—no matter how inexperienced the doctor might be. Some of my Navajo patients even brought me gifts when they came for their appointments. The gifts included various homemade foods, paintings, Navajo jewelry, and little hand-made weavings.

The University of New Mexico medical program recognized the value of these kinds of third-world, fly-by-the-seat-of-your-pants experiences that were routine at the Cuba Health Center. Medical students and residents aspiring to be rural doctors vied for the coveted opportunity to apprentice there. Mentoring these eager students and residents provided me with some of the most rewarding experiences I had during my stay in Cuba.

Toward the end of my two-year commitment, UNM offered me a position as assistant professor for its residency program in family medicine. It puzzled me that UNM would want to hire someone to teach who was only two years out of residency. Apparently the faculty viewed the Cuba experience as worth a decade of experience elsewhere.

One of the professors in the family medicine program said that the school had been searching for female role models for their student doctors and residents. With enthusiasm, I signed the contract and planned to move to Albuquerque when my two years of service in Cuba were up.

CHAPTER 18

State of Siege

Although I felt like I was in an unrelenting state of siege much of the time, helping women deliver their babies gave me a happy reprieve and was one of the highlights of my Cuba experience. Over the course of two years, I delivered almost 200 babies. Even in my chronically sleep-deprived state, participating in the births filled me with a kind of primal joy.

On some occasions, other emotions—like fear and anxiety—preceded the joy that came from delivering babies. Sometimes a foot or a hand appeared in the vaginal canal and not the baby's crowning head. Other times, the baby's heart slowed to a dangerously low rate, perhaps because the umbilical cord had become tightly wrapped around the baby's neck before birth.

Many of the mothers had not come in for prenatal visits, which could have helped us detect and address breach positions and other complications well before delivery. The Cuba Health Center was not equipped for major surgery such as C-sections. With most deliveries imminent at the time of the mother's arrival at the Health Center, evacuations to Albuquerque were out of the question. We had to improvise and pray for the best.

When a baby presented in a breach position at the time of delivery, it was customary for the staff to make phone contact with one of the seasoned obstetricians at the Indian Health Service Hospital many miles away in Gallup. An especially compassionate physician at the Indian Hospital, Dr. Waxman, agreed to be on standby for Cuba's obstetrical emergencies involving Native Americans. On speakerphone, Dr. Waxman's calm voice walked me through many difficult deliveries until I gained the confidence to handle them on my own.

One memorable occasion of obstetrical terror is engraved permanently in the archives of my mind. The baby's head delivered, but the body did not follow. The size of the baby's shoulders blocked its passage. No amount of maneuvering could relieve the obstruction. The baby showed signs of distress, with deceleration of the heart rate. The emergency transport helicopter team from the University of New Mexico had been notified and would soon be in the air. In spite of the urgency, the neonatal team did not arrive in time to help with the delivery.

By a stroke of luck, one of the nurses in the delivery room got through to Dr. Waxman. His comforting voice flowed out of the speakers on the wall in the delivery room.

"Okay, Erica. First of all, I want you to remember to breathe. We'll get through this together. Ready? Now slide your hands down both sides of the neck until your thumbs reach the collarbones. Do you feel them? Press on those bones until they snap. We're going to break the clavicles so we can bring in the shoulders toward the midline and deliver the rest of the body."

One of the aides held the Navajo mother's hand throughout the entire ordeal, as the mother remained stoically silent. I wondered what she was thinking and feeling.

A wave of nausea and light-headedness came over me as I felt the little bones break in my hands. I did exactly what Dr. Waxman said and moved the shoulders midline. With some gentle pulling, the baby eventually slid out of the vaginal canal and required only brief resuscitative efforts.

By the time the emergency transport team arrived to fly the baby to the newborn intensive care unit in Albuquerque, the baby girl was already out of danger and breathing on her own. With the helicopter back in the air heading south, I let tears of joy and relief flow as I held the new mom's hands in mine.

Two months later, the mother brought her baby girl in for her first well-child checkup. The baby looked vigorous and active. There was a bony callous at the midpoint of each clavicle, the only reminder of that perilous night.

It was tough staying up night after night doing deliveries. There were stretches of time when I was the only doctor available because the temporary doctor was on vacation or out job hunting.

When the temporary doctor, Bill, eventually resigned, I became the medical director by default, in addition to all my other duties. That position involved working with the administrator from Santa Fe, who was under intense pressure from governmental agencies to get the Health Center up to certain standards and in compliance with national hospital regulations. The Health Center was so marginal—understaffed, under-equipped, disorganized—that it would require a miracle to pass the site inspection.

The added responsibilities I assumed as medical director followed me relentlessly, even through my own emergency hospitalization.

On one of my weekends off duty, I went white-water canoeing in the nearby wilderness with my trusty canoe. I invited a friend who claimed he had ample experience canoeing in Class II and III water.

Halfway down the river, my friend asked to switch positions with me so he could steer the canoe from the stern. In spite of my doubts, I agreed to switch.

We beached the canoe, switched positions, and then pushed the canoe back into the water. A few minutes later, the canoe capsized in a particularly turbulent stretch of water. Pinned under the canoe, I was dragged by the current for a few yards over submerged rocks before I could extricate myself. When I came up for air, I saw that my left index finger was fractured and partially severed at the joint, hanging on by a strip of skin and torn tendons.

My friend helped me tightly bandage the ends together and then set up camp. I spent a sleepless, painful night beside the river. The next morning we paddled to a place downriver where I could seek help.

By the time we were able to get to the takeout place on the river, my hand was infected and I had a high fever and chills. After I was hospitalized overnight at the Cuba Health Center, the EMTs transferred me by ambulance to Presbyterian Hospital in Albuquerque, where a hand surgeon evaluated me. Eventually, after the infection resolved, the hand surgeon was able to successfully re-attach and save the mangled finger.

During my five days in the hospital, while feverish and on intravenous antibiotics, wondering if I would lose my finger, I received phone calls several times a day from the PMS administrator assigned to the Cuba Health Center. Despite my condition, he insisted on discussing business and asked repeatedly when I would be back at work, saying that PMS needed me back at the Health Center as soon as possible.

In those days, I hadn't yet learned to set clear boundaries for self-preservation. Early in my medical training, I had prayed that I might be of service to others. I failed to pray that I might be of service to myself as well. But by the time I completed my National Health Service obligation in Cuba, I was well on my way to being cured of this oversight.

After a week in the hospital as a patient, I went back to work with a cast on my hand and forearm, bracing myself for my multiple roles as physician in the clinic, ER doctor, and medical director of the Cuba Health Center.

Working at the Health Center was unsustainable by anyone's standards. The fatigue was crushing, with no chance of real recuperation. Sometimes I was so tired that I would succumb to a series of micro-naps with my eyes open—periods in which my brain repeatedly disengaged for a fraction of a second. Needless to say, this half-awake condition posed a potential threat to me and to others.

Early one evening, after being on duty for 36 hours, I drove to the convenience store across the road to get gas for my pickup truck. After pumping the gas, I drove off and within seconds rammed my truck into a concrete post that stood directly in front of me. My eyes were open, but I was having one of my unintentional micro-naps. The crash gave me the resolve to do something about my situation. I could no longer continue in this sleep-deprived manner, no matter how committed and conscientious I was.

In desperation, I telephoned the National Health Service office in Washington, D.C., and spoke to one of their officials. I related my plight, including my concern that I might inadvertently harm someone by making a mistake from sheer exhaustion—like writing the wrong medication or the wrong dose on a prescription pad.

I boldly asked for a transfer to a place with more help and humane conditions for the doctors. The official at the other end of the phone listened to me politely, but was unwavering in his position. "There's a serious shortage of doctors willing to serve in underserved areas. The Cuba Health Center needs you. They're in a somewhat desperate situation at the moment. You'll have to stay there until they can find some more long-term help."

I told the official I could not keep going anymore. He responded, "You just have to hang in there, Doctor. If you quit, under current policy you would owe the government three times the amount of the original loan, plus interest." When I asked if I had any other options, the official cited jail as a possibility. I insisted there must be another viable alternative. "Well, the only other options for leaving Cuba early are dying or being declared insane." I couldn't tell if his concluding statements were said in jest or in all seriousness.

After hanging up, I called Leonard Cain, the doctor who had informed me that he and all the other physicians had resigned in protest. We had stayed in touch. In my desperate state, I discussed the possibility of declaring insanity. He advised against it but had no other suggestions.

I almost called in sick one day to get some much-needed rest, but when I thought about all the people who needed help, my conscience propelled me out of bed. Besides, if the patients didn't see me in the clinic, there was always the possibility that they would come looking for me. Although most of my Navajo patients lived in remote areas far from town, it was not unusual for them to drive out to my house on my days off, looking for help.

At the clinic, one never knew what to expect. Doctoring was full of surprises—including pleasant ones. One day a friendly, attractive man named Tom Dwyer came into the clinic for an appointment. Tom worked with the Forest Service and had been assigned to the Cuba Ranger Station. He came in to be checked for a chronically painful ankle.

Normally oblivious to romantic attractions while in my professional on-duty demeanor, this time I felt unmistakable sparks as I held Tom's ankle during the examination and looked into his face as we spoke. We started spending time with each other. We were both lonely.

In spite of the challenges my work posed, developing a relationship with Tom seemed irresistible. Who would have guessed the role he would play in my future life?

CHAPTER 19

Road Man

Spring 1988

One evening, after a long day at work, I lay stretched out on the futon couch in my adobe home and stared out the large picture window at the sinking sun in the western sky. My tired mind tried to digest the events of the past 36 hours.

A fiery orange glow appeared in the sky above the Jemez Mountains as twilight slid slowly into darkness in the high desert of northern New Mexico. The scent of incense from the cedar and piñon logs in the wood-burning stove wafted throughout the house.

While lost in my reverie, I heard the rumble of a vehicle toiling up my long, rutted driveway. A horn honked. I waited in suspense—but no one came to the house.

Using all my force of will to rise up from the comfort of the couch, I opened the door and peered out into the fading light. Through swirls of settling dust, I saw a familiar maroon pickup truck parked a few yards away.

Dennison Begay and his wife sat motionless in the truck. I had delivered two of their babies at the Cuba Health Center. Dennison was a highly respected Road Man, an elder who leads peyote ceremonies in the Native American Church.

The couple waited for me to come outside and invite them into my home. This was a Navajo custom that originated from traditional life in remote and isolated hogans, where a sudden knock on the door could startle and frighten the people inside—especially if it was dark outside.

I beckoned the couple to come inside. I offered each of them a chair next to the wood stove. We sat opposite each other in the dimly lit living room.

Jet-black hair framed Dennison's chiseled face. He had high cheekbones and a ruddy-brown complexion. He wore a plaid shirt with a bolo tie, tight jeans held up by a finely tooled leather belt with a big silver buckle, and polished cowboy boots. Dennison sat on the edge of the chair with his back straight, creating a look of quiet dignity.

His wife, Lena, wore her long, thick black hair pulled back into the traditional *tsii yeel,* the Navajo knot adorned with white yarn. She dressed in the customary style of Navajo women, with a dark blue velvet blouse and a light blue satin skirt, held in place by a red-and-white woven sash around her slender waist and a glistening silver concho belt on top. Thin white socks and tennis shoes covered her feet.

Lena and Dennison were friendly but talked very little. Their eyes looked downward except when they spoke, a common trait among traditional Navajos.

The wood crackled in the stove. The mournful wailing of a lone coyote in the distance punctuated the long stretches of silence.

I sensed that they had something important on their minds, and that they needed to tell me in their own time. I waited and let myself enter into the timelessness of the Navajo, not an easy task given my irrepressible curiosity.

After an interminable silence, I jumped up and made them some tea. We engaged in short bursts of small talk, followed by more silence and staring at the floor. After a half-hour had passed, exhaustion overcame me. I thanked them for coming to my house and asked if there was anything they needed from me before they left.

Dennison began to speak in his slow and measured way. "My wife and I came because my people want to give you a gift to show our appreciation for your service to the Navajo people. We want to have an all-night peyote ceremony for you. In the ceremony, my people will pray that you will stay at the Cuba Health Center and continue your good work here for many more years."

Dennison knew that I had participated in the Native American Church ceremonies quite a few times in my younger years as a schoolteacher on the Navajo reservation.

Feeling surprised and touched, I enthusiastically accepted their gift. I smiled and shook their hands in the Navajo way, which meant our hands touched lightly for only a second or two. As they walked out the door, Dennison turned to tell me that he would let me know the time and place of the ceremony. I collapsed onto my bed and fell into a comatose-like sleep.

The morning came, accompanied by feelings of anxiety and doom. My heart pounded and I felt short of breath.

Did Dennison Begay really say that he and his people were going to pray for me to stay at the Cuba Health Center for many more years? I cannot let this happen. I need to do something.

Having witnessed and experienced the power of prayer in other peyote ceremonies in the past, I knew this prayer must be stopped. The thought of extending my stay at the Cuba Health Center filled me with apprehension.

After work, I drove to Dennison's house.

How can I tell Dennison that I don't want to stay in Cuba without seeming ungrateful for his generosity?

One of his kids answered the door. When Dennison appeared in the doorway, I stumbled over my words until I finally blurted out the truth. "Dennison, I can't accept your kind offer for the ceremony. I don't want to stay in Cuba. I can't. I signed a contract to teach at a medical training program for doctors in Albuquerque. I must leave Cuba. I'm sorry to let you and your people down."

Dennison did not reveal any emotion. He said, "We still want to give you the ceremony as our way of saying thank you for what you have done for our people. Just tell me what you want us to pray for."

Without taking the time to ponder my answer to his question, I replied, "I would like you to pray for my peace and happiness."

Peace and happiness are abstract concepts. Navajos are typically more concrete in their thinking. I had no idea how those two words would be translated into the Navajo way of thought.

The ceremony was planned for the following weekend. The temporary doctor agreed to be on call for me.

The Road Man had chosen a beautiful site among red rock formations, far from habitation. The weather was warm and windy and the skies were clear, except for occasional clumps of cumulus clouds that drifted across the sky.

The ceremony took place in a teepee, a custom borrowed from the Plains Indians. Navajo members of the Native American Church used teepees only during the warm months of the year.

About 25 Navajo men and women came to participate, some of whom I recognized from the clinic. We sat in a large circle with the sacred fire in the center. Heartfelt prayers and songs filled the night. We chewed on the peyote and drank the tea—the sacred "medicine" used to enhance the intensity of the prayers and allow us to enter into an altered state of consciousness where anything is possible.

The participants gave ardent speeches with expressions of their appreciation for my medical service and for being kind and respectful to their people. The ceremony was conducted in Navajo with a sprinkling of English words here and there. The name of Jesus was invoked frequently in the prayers.

While in a dream-like state, I heard Dennison, the Road Man, asking the participants to pray for me to have a baby, land, a home, and a husband—in that order. In that moment, I realized how he had interpreted my vague request for "peace and happiness."

I chewed on the four things that were mentioned. It sounded fascinating, but not at all possible, given my circumstances. Although Tom Dwyer and I were involved, we had no plans for marriage. I was two months short of turning 40. I had already made a resolute decision to accept my childless state if the circumstances weren't right for getting pregnant by the time I turned 40. On top of that, I didn't have any savings to buy land and a home. And besides, I had already signed a contract to teach in Albuquerque at the UNM Medical School family medicine program.

When it was my turn to pray, I thanked everyone for their prayers and their expressions of appreciation. And I shared with them how important the Navajo people had been in my life, especially in the early years after college.

Two months later, a few days before my fortieth birthday, I became pregnant with my son, Barrett. It was a conception against all odds and happened at an unlikely time in my very predictable cycle when pregnancies wouldn't normally occur.

The pregnancy coincided with the completion of my tour of duty in Cuba. I gave up my teaching opportunity with UNM and followed

Tom to his new assignment in the Pecos Ranger District several miles south of Santa Fe. I felt a lot of ambivalence about walking away from such a coveted position, but I was certain that I did not want to commute the 80 miles each way to Albuquerque and back while pregnant and later with a newborn baby.

Six months after the peyote ceremony, Tom and I purchased a couple of acres of land outside of Santa Fe and began building our home.

Nine months after the ceremony, we went to the courthouse and got married. I was six months pregnant.

In less than a year after the ceremony, I had a baby, land, a home, and a husband—in that order, the same order voiced in the prayer of the Road Man.

I got the Navajo version of peace and happiness. The Road Man's powerful prayers miraculously changed the course of my life with the birth of my son—the most amazing blessing I could ever have imagined.

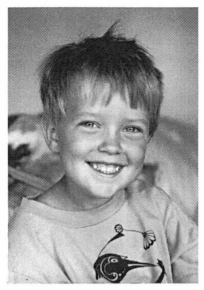

My son, Barrett, when he was four years old

EPILOGUE

Summer 2018

Much of what I knew and cherished about my life on the reservation has disappeared from view, but still remains in my journals and photographs, on my cassette tapes—and in the fiber of my soul.

On my most recent visit to Chinle, I drove to the abandoned housing compound where I had lived as a schoolteacher. The duplex apartment looked tiny, dingy, and overgrown with weeds—without a hint of ever having housed a happy young schoolteacher filled with gratitude to be among the Navajo people.

Marshall and I remained friends until his death from pneumonia in 2007. He was 85. He lived most of his adult life devoted to his people. I am still in touch with his two grown children, Deswood and Dana (formerly "Desbah") Tome. They are both following in their father's footsteps in their commitment to serving the Navajo people. I hope to meet Marshall's three grandchildren someday. One is an up-and-coming Native filmmaker.

Over the years, I have passed through Chinle several times on my way to Canyon de Chelly. The Chinle of today is very different from when I lived there. Most of the roads are paved. The little town has mushroomed and now has a hospital, a shopping center, restaurants, and motels. Like elsewhere in the States, the people eat more junk food and don't look as healthy as they did decades earlier. The slim, strong men and women I remember are less numerous. Many of the children I encounter are not able to speak Navajo and no longer follow the traditional ways of their grandparents.

While saddened by feelings of loss, at the same time I feel heartened to see that there is a growing movement within the younger generations to carry on the traditional ceremonies. Many Navajo artists, writers, filmmakers, and activists are taking the culture into new and exciting places.

Life among the Navajo decades ago felt both foreign and familiar at the same time—as though I were re-living a past life when I was a Navajo woman who had returned to her spiritual home.

For many years after I left the reservation, I refrained from speaking or writing about the magic and mystery of those times, not wanting to face the skepticism I would encounter from Anglo people.

During a moment of camaraderie in medical school, I told my classmates about the miraculous healings I had witnessed during the peyote ceremonies, including the instant healing of sick babies and the spontaneous disappearance of the suspiciously enlarged and rock-hard lymph node under my chin. I even mentioned my momentary ability to speak fluent Navajo—and recite prayers and sing songs I had never heard before—while under the influence of the mind-altering plant medicine.

When my classmates laughed and dismissed my stories as something I had imagined, I remembered what the Road Man had said when he "read" my mind. "No, they won't believe you. You don't need to talk about it to anyone."

Through the power of their rituals and ceremonies, the traditional Navajo people had access to a dimension that was no longer recognized by white people, but that was clearly as real as ever. Some people would call what I witnessed "miracles," because there was no rational explanation for their occurrence.

I saw quite a few miracles during my time among the Navajo people. The biggest miracle I experienced, though, was the birth of my son—prayed for in the peyote ceremony—a conception against all odds.

The Navajo children in my classroom made a profound difference in my life. From the moment I attempted to learn their language and see the world through their eyes, a transformation took place within me. I went from wanting to quit my job and escape the reservation to falling madly in love with the kids in my class, their land, and their culture. The children and their families opened their hearts to me. They invited me into their homes and their sacred ceremonies, and they shared with me the richness of their traditional lives.

My life as a sheepherder allowed me to glimpse what it feels like to see the world through the eyes of a Navajo. I got to understand and appreciate people from a different world than the world I had grown up in. This understanding grew into empathy and love, and a feeling that my heart was part Navajo—biological facts notwithstanding.

My experience among the Navajo people has influenced the rest of my life—including how I practice medicine. In addition to learning about the power of empathy to repair misunderstandings and heal the heart, I discovered the power of plants to heal the body. Herbal medicine—along with healthy nutrition—are two of the most important tools for recovering from chronic medical conditions.

I also learned about the importance of living in harmony with one's community and with the land, what the traditional Navajos call "walking in beauty." Most important of all, I learned that healing can take place against all odds.

When my patients are struggling and don't know what to do regarding treatment—even though they have all the facts—I tell them to consult with the wise part of themselves that knows exactly what's in their best interest. To access their own innate wisdom, I urge my patients to go to a deep and quiet place within—free of fear—and ask for help and guidance.

During my medical training in Denver, a close friend gave me a gift certificate to consult with a local psychic. I had never been to a psychic before and didn't know what to expect.

The psychic told me to bring to the session any questions I wanted answered. I couldn't think of anything in particular to ask her, probably because I didn't know if psychic readings had any validity.

A few minutes after I walked into the psychic's home office and sat down, the psychic said she could see that I already had someone with whom I could consult about anything that was on my mind.

"Who is that person you're talking about?" I asked with skepticism.

"She's the wise old lady standing behind you. She looks like a Navajo grandmother. She's always with you." These words left me speechless, with much to ponder.

One of the traditional Navajo prayers, called *Walking in Beauty*, is the closing prayer from the healing ceremony called the *Blessing Way*, designed to restore harmony in the cosmos.

The Navajo word *hózhó* is loosely translated into English as *beauty*. But this word means far more than beauty. For the Navajo, *hózhó* conveys an important concept in their religion and refers to a sense of happiness, peace, well-being, wisdom, balance, and harmony. Traditional Navajos continually restore balance in their daily lives, both with the mundane and the divine.

Traditional Navajos believe that when people get sick, it is because they are no longer in harmony with the world. The Blessing Way ceremony removes the imbalance and restores the sick person to *hózhó*. The ceremony lasts several days and involves a medicine man who knows all the songs, prayers, and sand paintings required to complete the ritual.

The Blessing Way is designed to attract the "holy people," who will reconnect the sick people with their heritage and the beauty all around them and to *hózhó*.

Hózhóogo naasháa doo
Shitsijí' hózhóogo naasháa doo
Shikéédéé hózhóogo naasháa doo
Shideigi hózhóogo naasháa doo
T'áá altso shinaagóó hózhóogo naasháa doo
Hózhó náhásdlíí'
Hózhó náhásdlíí'
Hózhó náhásdlíí'
Hózhó náhásdlíí'
In beauty I walk
With beauty before me I walk
With beauty behind me I walk
With beauty above me I walk
With beauty around me I walk
It has become beauty again
It has become beauty again
It has become beauty again
It has become beauty again

AFTERWORD

Medicine and Miracles in the High Desert is the first of a series of four memoirs that I am working on. The remaining books in the series will be about the unusual twists and turns along the road to finding my life's purpose, the decade I spent as a doctor practicing strictly Western medicine, the health catastrophe I experienced that opened up a whole new world of healing—off the path of mainstream medicine—and my medical detective work in helping patients recover from mysterious illnesses.

When the mountain lion sniffed me inches away from my face as I lay in my sleeping bag, I sensed that this close encounter had some sort of hidden meaning. The grandmother of one of my Navajo friends told me that the mountain lion was my spirit guide and had come to give me "his courage, strength, and intense focus," because I would need those for what lay ahead. She said that I would face many obstacles, some big and life-threatening, and if I lived through them, I would have "a strong heart and powerful medicine to give to the people."

True to prophecy, the challenges I had to overcome in order to fulfill my life's purpose led to profound insights that both deepened my humanity and helped me to be a better doctor. I am writing these stories and sharing them after all these years in hopes that they might inform and inspire readers like you.

ABOUT THE AUTHOR

Erica Elliott lives in Santa Fe, New Mexico, where she has a busy medical practice. She is a founding member of The Commons, a co-housing community where she has lived happily since 1993 and where she raised her son, Barrett Dwyer.

Throughout her childhood, Erica moved frequently with her family due to her father's work. She began her schooling in England, graduated from high school in Germany, and studied art history in Italy. She returned to the States to earn her undergraduate degree at Antioch College.

After college, Erica spent time in Switzerland learning more about her uncle, an eccentric and brilliant medical doctor. She went on to teach grade school on the Navajo Reservation, followed by time in Ecuador with the Peace Corps. She honed her mountaineering skills by snow and ice climbing in the Andes, instructing Outward Bound students in rock climbing and wilderness survival, and leading an all-women's expedition to the top of Denali in Alaska. During this phase of her life, she also studied the spiritual practices of Indigenous cultures.

After graduating from University of Colorado Medical School and completing her residency in family practice in Denver, Erica began her medical career in an understaffed health clinic in Cuba, New Mexico. From there, she served in a variety of healthcare settings, including a clinic for indigent care, a busy emergency room, a women's clinic, and a multispecialty clinic.

In 1993, Erica opened her own private practice in her co-housing community. Known as "the Health Detective," she specializes in treating mysterious and difficult-to-diagnose illnesses.

Erica's unrelenting curiosity has led her on many eye-opening and heart-opening adventures. The years she spent living in foreign cultures, both as a child and an adult, have enabled her to bring a fresh perspective to her life's work.

Erica blogs about her life and medical insights at www.musingsmemoirandmedicine.com.

Printed in the United States
By Bookmasters